The annual Talent Education National Concert, held in Tokyo on March 28, 1980, had 3500 participants.

Shinichi Suzuki:
The Man and His Philosophy

by Evelyn Hermann

A Senzay. Edition
by Ability Development Associates, Inc.
subsidiary of Accura Music
Athens, Ohio, U.S.A.

ISBN: 0-918194-07-5
Library of Congress Catalog Card Number: LC 80-67542
Jacket Design: Paul Bradford
Lithographed in the United States of America by
Lawhead Press, Inc., Athens, Ohio.

Dedication

To Shinichi Suzuki, who has devoted his
lifetime to the happiness of all children. He
seeks to awaken in them an awareness of beauty
and a respect for life through musical perception. Everyone he reaches receives new insights
into the great potential of each individual and
the ways in which man might live in peace.

Acknowledgements

The author wishes to express her gratitude to Mrs. Waltraud Suzuki. Without her willing assistance this work would not have been possible.

I wish to express additional thanks to all those colleagues and friends who contributed photographs, helped in verifying dates, and assisted in recalling the details in this book.

To my mother I am grateful for the opportunity to study music which led me to know Shinichi Suzuki.

Table of Contents

PART 2   SHINICHI SUZUKI: HIS PHILOSOPHY

ix

Table of Illustrations

Shinichi Suzuki:
The Man

Prologue

As the train leaves Shinjuku station in Tokyo, it signals its departure with a little "music box" folk tune. For the first hour of our three and one-half hour train ride, we are still within the city limits of Tokyo. Then the houses become fewer, and the orchards and the rice paddies appear.

Japan is a rugged land of high mountains, deep valleys, and many small plains. Only 13 percent of the land is arable. The trip to Matsumoto takes us through the scenic Japan Alps, so named because of the grandeur of its landscape. After leaving the foothills, we travel through a seemingly endless series of tunnels, each of which shows us another valley or small plain where the people have worked all of the tillable land, in many cases extending their cultivation halfway up the mountain slopes. Each series of tunnels takes us to a higher elevation as the train wends its way to central Honshu. After about three hours, we come to the final tunnel series and emerge on the outer rim of a rather large valley. We slowly descend into the valley city of Matsumoto, and as a signal to the passengers that the end of the line is near, we again hear the "music box" folk tune.

Matsumoto has grown from a hidden isolated village to a thriving community since the 1940s. The national winter Olympics of 1977-78 opened the city of 100,000 to all Japanese; but during the late 1960s, a quiet Japanese violin teacher brought Matsumoto to the attention of the musical world.

As we leave the railroad station and walk straight ahead from the front exit, we see the tower of NHK, Japan's national radio and television station. It is only a short walk to the studios, which are located on the perimeter of a small, landscaped square. Next to the station is a very contemporary building with the western title, "Talent Education Institute." This is the home of the Suzuki method and philosophy, and it houses the offices and classrooms of Dr. Shinichi Suzuki and his teachers. On the lower level of the building is a pre-school with children ranging in age from three to six. Some are practicing calligraphy, others are writing numbers, and all have the skill of a teenager. Orientals, who can read the calligraphy of these young people, remark how brilliant these students are. We are told that they eventually will learn 200 *Haiku* poems, and by the time they are ready for school, many will have raised their I.Q. by as much as 30 points.

From a corner room come the sounds of an accomplished pianist. Opening the door, we see a very small child playing a Mozart sonata with the maturity and understanding of an adult.

In the distance, the sounds of violins fill the hall. The musical sound is similar to the violin music heard in the great conservatories of Europe and the United States in the 1950s. Going up the stairs and into the studios, we find that all the beautiful sounds are being produced by very young children, from four to six years of age. We cannot believe our eyes. First, a six year old plays the Bach *A minor Concerto,* then a seven year old plays Mozart's *D Major Concerto.* Finally, an eight year old plays Kreisler's *Preludium and Allegro.* It is quite an emotional experience for a first-time visitor.

Leaving these young musicians, we come to another room from which we hear a cacophony formed from parts of three concertos. Opening the doors, we are surprised to find three older students, and upon inquiry we are told they are *kenkyusai* (student teachers) from such faraway places as Australia, France, and England. They have come to Matsumoto to study with Dr. Suzuki. Because there is a shortage of practice areas, these students have learned to practice simultaneously in one room.

The hallway leads us to a corner door and the studio of Suzuki *Sensei*,[1] who is responsible for all of the various activities in the Talent Education Institute. In other parts of the world, we would refer to these young people as geniuses; however, Suzuki does not believe in genius. He feels that anyone can be brought to the level of accomplishment found here, and he often states, "Any child can be educated." His aim in life is to bring this message to the entire world. Many areas have already begun to use his approach to teach music to small children. Now he is turning his attention to education in general.

---

[1]*Sensei* — beloved and revered teacher.

Chapter 1

Man is the Son of His Environment

(1859-1919)

Background

To understand the man Suzuki and his philosophy, one must understand his environment. Five hundred years prior to 1867, Japan was a feudal country governed by the strongest warlord, or *Shogun*. The *Shogun's* warriors, or *samurai*, were an elite group highly trained in the skills of protecting their *Shogun*. The breakdown of the *Shogunate* began in the 1850s, when a series of treaties made trade possible with other countries. By 1860, there was a Japanese Embassy in the United States and two years later, they had opened embassies in several European countries.

In 1866, the *Shogunate* of Tokugawa, Toshinobu, came into power; but almost immediately there was a move to restore the power of the emperor. One year later, the 15 year old Emperor Meiji became ruler. Most of his ministers were of the *samurai* class, because these people had been trained in the tradition of responsibility and leadership.

Many members of the *samurai* class fell into a period of great depression because they had learned only one

Ryo Fujie Suzuki, mother of Shinichi Suzuki

skill — war. However, those who had the foresight to seek an education in other fields of endeavor found new lives. In 1872, Emperor Meiji, the "Enlightened Emperor," published an Imperial decree for the encouragement of education; in part, the decree stated:

> There shall, hereafter, be no illiterate family among the people of any community, nor shall there be an illiterate member of any family . . . learning is the basis for all human endeavor from the commonplace — speaking, reading, writing, and calculating for everyday needs — to the professional need of the military man, government official, farmer, merchant, craftsman, and artist, in the multitude of technical skills and arts, and in the law, politics, and astronomy.[1]

By 1912, when the Emperor died, the goal of the decree had become a reality.

The first educational institution, Tokyo University, was opened in 1877, and within 30 years, four other universities were established. The country, which had been an isolated feudal state 60 years before, had become one of the great powers of the modern world.

It was during this era of change that the parents of Shinichi Suzuki were married and raised their family. The mother, Ryo Fujie, was the daughter of a *samurai* family. Her father was independently wealthy, and she was well-educated to the Meiji standards for young girls. She attended a singing school where she learned Japanese songs and *samisen*[2] playing, Ikebana and Ocha ceremony, and other Japanese cultural arts. She married at the age of 18.

Suzuki's father, Masakichi, was born in 1859 to Masaharu, a *samurai* of some standing. Masaharu had taken up the trade of *samisen* making. At the age of 10, Masakichi was sent to an English school for two years;

---

[1]Bradley Smith, *Japan: A History in Art* (New York: Doubleday & Co., 1964), 286-7.
[2]*Samisen* — a Japanese three-stringed instrument.

Masakichi Suzuki, father of Shinichi Suzuki

at the age of 14, he began working for his father, making *samisens*. In 1877, at the age of 18, as was the custom in those days, he became head of the family.

By 1886, business had declined and Masakichi, who was now 28 years old, attended a *Shihan* School (Japanese song school). He wanted to become an English teacher, which indicates his pioneer spirit, since only a few years earlier their country had been isolated. All of that changed, however, when Masakichi saw and heard his first violin.

The violin had been known in Japan, but with the persecution of the Christians by the Tokugawas, it was no longer heard. The reign of Emperor Meiji brought it back into use once again, and by chance, Shinichi's father found an instructor in a teachers college who had a violin. Masakichi sought the teacher's permission to take the violin home overnight, and while he had it, he made a drawing of the instrument.

In 1888 he made his first violin, and a year later he began selling violins to Nihon Gakki, a well-known Japanese music company. By 1900 Masakichi opened the Suzuki Violin Factory in Nagoya, and a few years later they began making mandolins and guitars.

During this period, the Suzukis were raising their family. Umeo, the first son, was born in 1889; Hana, the first daughter, was born three years later. Shinichi, the third son, was born in October, 1898. In all, the Suzuki family grew to seven sons and five daughters. The children were brought up in the violin factory, and when they had childish squabbles, they would hit one another with violins, for they thought of the violin as a sort of toy.

During the time of the Russo-Japanese War of 1904-5, those people who did the manual work of polishing the tops and backs of the violins usually worked at night under an oil lamp that hung from the ceiling. Shinichi used to listen spellbound as these workmen would tell him tales of Japanese heroes. In fine storytelling

fashion, just as they would get to the climax they would
stop and say, "Now, a rice cake would taste good," and
Shinichi would run home and get pieces of *mochi* (rice
cake) from a big keg in the kitchen. The storyteller would
toast the *mochi* cake over a brazier, and again, as he
polished his violins, he would take up where he left off
with the story.

During this first decade of the 20th century, the
violin factory prospered. By 1908, Masakichi became a
member of the National Assembly. In 1910, he went to
England for five months, and also toured other European
countries. By this time the factory was producing 65,800
violins per year, and had become the largest factory in
the world. They produced fine, machine-made instruments, and it is said, if he had had good wood, his bows
would have rivaled those made by the fine European
bow makers. Masakichi never stopped his study and research to improve what he was doing. This ongoing study
was obviously the pattern by which Shinichi has lived,
for even today he is continually researching his teaching
methods.

Suzuki Enters Commercial School

In 1912, the Emperor Meiji died, and Emperor
Taisho came to power. In 1913, a representative of the
Emperor visited the factory, which was now enlarged
to 600 *tsubo* (one *tsubo* is two *tatami*).[3] The factory by
now was employing 270 workers, and it was during this
time that Suzuki's father sent him to a commercial school
in Nagoya because he wanted him to be able to handle
factory business in the future. During the summer months
he would work in the factory to get a general idea of
violin production.

---

[3]Buildings in Japan are measured by the number of *tatami* mats that they
can put on the floor. *Tatami,* being of a regulation size, are 1.8 meters in
length by .9 meters wide.

Suzuki's father, Masakichi, proudly poses with his medal, The
Second Order of the Rising Sun, received from the Emperor.

While at this commercial school, Suzuki learned an important lesson in living. The motto of the school was "Character first, ability second," and these words were to become Suzuki's motto for life.

He was obviously a very popular person, because he was nominated president of his class for the entire four years he attended the school. One experience, which he remembers vividly, occurred during a final examination just before graduation. One student was cheating on the exam, and another student loudly reported it to the teacher. The cheating student was immediately sent out of the room, but as soon as the informer left the room, the students who were waiting in the hall gave him a sound thrashing. Even though Suzuki was still in the room taking the exam, he was called into the faculty room because he was class president. In order to protect the students, he said he had also been involved in the fight. The teachers asked him if he thought it was right to cheat. He said no, but he also thought it was a breach of friendship to report the student who had cheated. Suzuki went back into the classroom and asked the class if they would all be willing to fail the exam, even if it meant coming back to school the fifth year. Even those who had nothing to do with the fight agreed to do so. To punish the class, they were all suspended. When Suzuki told his father the story and asked him to put him through school for another year because he was about to fail, his father smiled and said, "Well, it can't be helped, can it?" and Suzuki knew from the smile that his father agreed with him.

The recess lasted for about a week, and then the students were summoned to appear at school. All of the students gathered in the auditorium, and the man who had created the motto "First character, then ability," and whom Suzuki admired greatly, spoke to the students with tears in his eyes. He ended his talk by saying what had happened would all be forgotten, and the final exam would be given again. The class of 1916 graduated on time and in its entirety. There were no failures that year. After graduation, Suzuki entered the factory as a regular staff member in charge of the export section, packing and booking. It was a busy and happy time for him. In 1917, his father was decorated by the Emperor with the order of the Order of the Rising Sun for his outstanding work in violin production. In 1918, the factory was again enlarged. Production reached a peak of 500 violins daily, and there were now 1200 employees. Masakichi built a new family home with beautiful landscaping and an exceptionally beautiful garden in Tashirocho, Nagoya.

The Marquis Tokugawa

After about two years of work in the factory, Shinichi developed a slight fever which occurred each evening, and the doctor suggested that he rest. In late autumn, 1918, he went to an inn at Okitsu for three months to recuperate, and, while there, he met the Yanagida family. Mr. Yanagida, his wife, and two small children had come from Hokaido, and since Suzuki loved children, they soon became friends. Mr. Yanagida told Suzuki that he had been a schoolmate of the Marquis Tokugawa, and shortly after Suzuki returned to Nagoya, he received a letter from Mr. Yanagida asking him if he would like to become a member of an expedition led by the Marquis Tokugawa, that was going to the island of Chishima for one month of biological research. Though not a researcher, Suzuki was to enjoy the sightseeing around the islands. The ship was scheduled to sail on August 1st, and Suzuki's father agreed that he might accept the invitation, so Suzuki went to Tokyo to get the Marquis' approval. There he met Mr. Tokugawa for the first time, a meeting which was to decide his entire fate, and to lead his life into a new direction.

Influence of Tolstoy and Dogan

Prior to this meeting with the Marquis Tokugawa, two other people made a very strong impression on Suzuki. A story which he frequently tells to explain his philosophy relates that one day he discovered an English typewriter in his father's office, and he started punching the keys. The chief of the export department came in and reprimanded him, saying that one must not type without putting paper in the machine. Suzuki promptly lied, saying that he really wasn't putting the keys down. "Oh, I see," replied the man. He was hardly out of sight when Suzuki was filled with anger against himself. It upset him so much that he couldn't bear it and went home. He could not sit still, and walked down the street to rid himself of the annoyance. He walked into a bookshop and spotted a copy of Tolstoy's *Diary* on a shelf. Opening the book, his eyes fell upon the following words: "To deceive oneself is worse than to deceive others." These words were a great shock to him, and he could scarcely control his emotions. He bought the book, and rushed home to read it from cover to cover. He reread the book so many times that it eventually fell apart. He carried the book everywhere he went. Tolstoy also wrote, "One should not deceive oneself and the voice of conscience is the voice of God," and Suzuki decided to live according to these principles.

Suzuki was not only influenced by Tolstoy at this age, but also by the priest, Dogan, for he diligently studied his works entitled *Shushogi,* which began, "It is the great Buddha Karma that illuminates life and lightens death: If the Buddha is in life and death, there is no life and death. . . ." About this time, Shinichi took up the study of Zen Buddhism seriously, and he studied with a great master who had only one other pupil. (The other pupil was to become mayor of Tokyo in the 1960s.) They studied about the great life force, and one's ability to control it. They developed this ability to the extent that they could hold hot coals in their hands. Suzuki also learned to use this ability to heal.

Many years later when Leonid Kogan, the great Russian violinist, came to Japan to concertize, he was having trouble with his arm. He had called in doctors to help him, but to no avail. Kogan was about to cancel his tour, when someone recommended they call Suzuki. Suzuki worked with him for a short time, and the artist was cured and able to continue his tour.

The great Zen master with whom Suzuki had studied was his mother's uncle, Fuzan Asano. He was a Senshu University professor, and later the head priest of Chuzenji Temple (O-Terra) with 400 temples. He became quite famous throughout Japan.

Daisetsu Suzuki's book, *What is Zen, states,*

> One of the characteristics of human life is experience. That is because he [man] remembers. Memory is an extremely precious thing, and the fact that he speculates and conceives ideas is due to his having a memory as a basis. Only because he has a memory is experience possible, and if experience is possible, how many ways of evolution are open to him. . . . With memory as the basis, he has experiences, and because of experience, he can reason.[4]

This writing has become the basis of learning in Talent Education. Suzuki believes that anyone can acquire this memory, and the greater the memory, the more developed the person will become.

Suzuki's father also had a very strong influence on his life. Shinichi says that when he was in middle school, there was a time when he and several neighborhood children used to visit the local shrine every evening. One day his father asked him what he said when he was visiting the shrine, and Shinichi replied that he asked for pro-

[4]Shinichi Suzuki, *Nurtured by Love* (Smithtown, New York: Exposition Press, 1969), pp. 103-4.

tection for the family. His father said, "Stop being selfish, when you go to the shrine each day, all you should say is 'Thank you very much.' "

From these studies of Tolstoy and Zen, Suzuki developed the belief that at about the age of 17, our future fate begins to unfold. He feels that our lives are managed from "over there" and that we here in this life gain nothing by worrying and fear, but should always have hope and live to the best of our abilities.

It must have been before I graduated from commercial college. Unexpectedly we got a gramophone. It was not electric, like the modern ones, but had to be wound by hand, and it had a horn as a loudspeaker. This horn was shaped like a morning-glory and was big enough for a child to put its head inside. The first record I bought was Schubert's "Ave Maria" played by Mischa Elman. The sweetness of the sound of Elman's violin utterly enthralled me. His velvety tone as he played the melody was like something in a dream. It made a tremendous impression on me. To think that the violin, which I had considered a toy, could produce such beauty of tone!

Elman's "Ave Maria" opened my eyes to music. I had no idea why my soul was so moved. But at least I had already developed the ability to appreciate this beauty. My profound emotion was the first step in my search for the true meaning of art. I brought a violin home from the factory, and listening to Elman playing a Haydn minuet, I tried to imitate him. I had no score, and simply moved the bow, trying to play what I heard. Day after day I did this, trying to master the piece. My complete self-taught technique was more scraping than anything else, but somehow I finally got so I could play the piece.

Haydn's minuet was thus my first "piece." Eventually I got so I derived great comfort from playing the violin, and became very fond of the instrument as well as developing deep love for music.[5]

---

[5]*Ibid,* pp. 78-9.

Chapter 2

Good Environmental Conditions Produce Superior Ability
(1919-1928)

The Voyage

In August of 1919, aboard the 1300 ton ship, *Chifu-Maru*, the expedition sailed to northern Chishima. There were 30 people aboard, including Mr. Tokugawa, Mr. Yanagida, members of the Tokugawa Biological Research Institute, and as guests Mrs. Matsudaira, a sister of Mr. Tokugawa; her son; Miss Nobu Koda, a renowned pianist; and Suzuki. (Miss Koda had joined the expedition in memory of her brother, who had been the first Japanese to set foot on the northern Chishima Islands.)

In August it was very cool in Chishima, and the atmosphere was clear. The sky was blue and the water was an even deeper blue. The wild flowers carpeted the grounds, and the scenery impressed all members of the expedition. It was a happy voyage. Shinichi's violin had by this time become a part of him, and since there was a piano on board, he was accompanied in his practice periods by Miss Koda. Since he was so young and inexperienced, it didn't occur to him to feel awkward as he played for Miss Koda, who was a fine pianist, and they played together many times while on board ship.

Encouragement to Study

That fall, after the cruise, the Marquis Tokugawa went to Nagoya to visit the Suzukis. While there he asked Masakichi what he thought about Shinichi studying violin, saying that Miss Koda had noted that the boy showed promise. Masakichi originally felt that musicians were obliged to "kowtow" to people in order to live. He felt that if Shinichi liked music, he could become a successful business man and then hire people to come play for him. Therefore, Shinichi was not sure how his father would feel about his studying music. However, when the Marquis asked, Masakichi could not say no. So the following spring, when Suzuki was 21, he went to Tokyo to study the rudiments of violin with Ko Ando, younger sister of Miss Koda. He was given a room in the Marquis Tokugawa's mansion in Fujimi-cho, Azabu. Suzuki planned originally to buy a house in which to live, but this plan didn't work out. Instead the Marquis invited him to stay in his mansion, which was a golden opportunity to associate with the Marquis and his colleagues. Suzuki became even closer to the Marquis, since he had his meals with him, and the Marquis told

A western style oil-on-canvas painting, circa 1910, by artist Sakaki Teitoku depicts an early use of violins with Japanese instruments.

Shinichi many things. The Marquis Tokugawa was one of the last descendents of the *Shoguns,* and almost every day there were important visitors and scholars visiting the Tokugawa mansion. The guests included physicist Torahiku Terada, and the phoneticist Kotoji Satsuda. Reflecting on this, Suzuki believes that this was the Marquis' way of seeing that his character was properly trained.

Suzuki had a lesson with Mrs. Ando every week, and later she suggested that perhaps the next year he should study at the Ueno Academy of Music. Suzuki began to prepare for the entrance exam, and as the examination day neared, he went to hear a graduation recital at Ueno. He was so disappointed that he talked to Mrs. Ando the next day, and said, "I do not want to take the entrance exam. I would rather go on studying with you, if I may." Mrs. Ando said that was alright, if that was what he preferred, but he would have to work hard. He started lessons with her again, and also studied music theory in private lessons with Professor Ryutaro Hirota, and acoustics with Professor H. Tanabe.

Because he did not enter the Academy, he had an even greater opportunity. After Suzuki had studied in Tokyo for about a year and one half, the Marquis Tokugawa began making plans for a world tour, and he asked, "Suzuki, why don't you come too. It will take about a year, and it will be fun."

> I had just started studying the violin. I thought I was a bit too young to benefit from a world tour at this stage of my life, and I said so. So the matter was dropped, and it was agreed that I should work hard at my violin. But soon after my summer vacation started, and one day, at home, I mentioned the proposed tour to my father. His reply was unexpected: "Why, that's an excellent idea." As I looked up he continued, "If you were with the Marquis, I shouldn't worry about you at all. It would be a good idea for you to have a look at the world. You

can probably go round the world for 150,000 yen. Go along and keep the Marquis company."[1]

Even at his father's urging, he still refused because he didn't want to give up his violin studies which he had just begun.

That September, after the holidays were over, one evening at dinner, I, Suzuki, told the Marquis what my father had said. Holding his chopsticks in midair, he looked at me with a twinkle in his eye. "Well done, Shinichi. You'd better grab the 150,000 yen. You can stop off in Germany and study violin. What a good idea!

Next time I go to Nagoya I'll have a word with your father."

Marquis Tokugawa completely sold my father on his ingenious scheme. He apparently said, "I am delighted that you will take my son with you, sir. By all means let him study in Germany with whatever money is left over."[2]

And so fate completely changed the life of Shinichi.

To Europe to Study

Tolstoy taught Suzuki meekness, but what had led him to Germany was the Marquis' great love. Because of his meekness and childlike ability to follow, the Marquis never failed to push him and give him the encouragement he needed.

By autumn Suzuki was sailing aboard the luxury liner, *Hakone Maru*, en route to Marseilles. His father thought he was on a world tour, but he was really on his way to Germany to study. It was October, 1920, and Shinichi was 22. Inflation was tremendous in Germany, so his money went a long way. When he first arrived, the exchange rate was 600 marks for 10 yen; and at the

1*Nurtured by Love*, pp. 82-3.
2*Ibid.*, p. 83.

end of his stay, he received 100,000,000 marks for 10 yen. It did cost him more than 150,000 yen though, because he spent eight years in Germany.

When the ship reached France, Suzuki said goodbye to the Marquis, and went straight to Berlin with a Mr. Fiegel, a German engineer that he had befriended on board the *Hakone Maru*. He took a room in a hotel, and for three months went to concerts every day. Professor Ando had offered Suzuki a letter of introduction to a teacher, but Suzuki had refused. He went to hear everybody from famous performers to rising young artists to find somebody that he could say, "This is the man I want for a teacher."

After three months, he was still looking, and he was about to move to Vienna when he heard a concert at the Sing Academy performed by the Klingler Quartet. The entire program was devoted to Mozart, and this event was to have a profound effect on his life and thought.

And when it came to the Clarinet Quintet (A Major, K. 581), something happened to me that had never happened before. I felt as though I had lost the use of my arms.

It was Mozart who taught me to know perfect love, truth, goodness and beauty. And I now deeply feel as if I were under the direct orders of Mozart, and he left me a legacy, and in his place I am to further the happiness of all children. What led to this revelation was the Klingler's Quartet playing of Mozart's Clarinet Quintet.

That evening I seemed to be gradually drawn into Mozart's spirit, and finally I was not conscious of anything else, not even my own being, I became so immersed. Of course, I did not realize this until afterward. After the performance I tried to clap. But there was no feeling from my shoulders down, and I could not move either hand. I didn't know when the clapping stopped. During the applause, I just sat there in a trance. Finally I got my hands back, but even when the feeling came back, I just stared into space. An indescribable, sublime, ecstatic joy had taken hold of my soul. I had been given a glimpse of Mozart's high spiritual world. Through sound, for the first time in my life I had been able to feel the highest pulsating beauty of the human spirit, and my blood burned within me. It was a moment of sublime eternity when I, a human being, had gone beyond the limits of this physical body. That night I couldn't sleep at all. Mozart, the man, had shown me immortal light. . . .

From that day until now, I have received power and strength from Mozart. . . . What I never cease to marvel at in Mozart's music is his superhuman love. It is a great tenderness and love felt only by the soul. And this love takes cognizance of man's deep sorrow . . . birth and death . . . and the evanescense and loneliness of life . . . the all-pervasive sadness. . . .

Mozart answers life with a loving affirmative. That is why it is possible to go beyond this despair, to envelop the situation in love and change it and bring about the joy of living.

When I listen to Mozart, he seems to envelop me in his great love. Mozart's love for mankind is not merely a pious kind of love that points to the hope in the next world through religious ecstasy: "All right, Life is sad. But, if there is love, see how beautiful life can be. The sad life that we all must live — let us go along together and comfort one another." This is what Mozart says to us, and I affirm it with all my heart.[3]

I can still vividly remember the sound of their performance that night. It was music of profound spirituality. It completely charmed my soul with its beauty, and it spoke to me gently. At the same time, it had superb order and technique. Without any introduction, and in English, since as yet I could not write German, I wrote [to Klingler], "Please take me as your pupil."[4]

---

[3]*Ibid.*, pp. 91-3.
[4]*Ibid.*, p. 84.

The Klingler String Quartet with Karl Klingler, Suzuki's teacher, at left as first violinist.

Suzuki Plays for Klingler

The young Japanese musicians greatly discouraged Suzuki, because they told him that Klingler did not take private pupils. However, the following Wednesday, he received an answer from Klingler, saying, "Come." And so he visited Klingler, who asked him to play the *Rode Concerto*. When Suzuki made an error, and had to play a passage again, he was certain Klingler would not accept him. When he was finished, Klingler said, "When can you come again?"

So now, for the first time, Suzuki had a teacher that he had chosen himself. At the time, Klingler was about 40 years of age, and he was a handsome man who had a very winning personality that endeared him to Suzuki. Suzuki was his only pupil, and Klingler delved into the compositions not only from the technical standpoint, but from the point of view of the composer when he was writing the works. For example, if they studied something of Handel, he would talk about the religious feeling that Handel must have had when he was writing. So Suzuki now learned not only the composition, but the character of the composer as well.

Klingler often had concerts in his home, and would invite Suzuki to come and listen. This again gave Suzuki more opportunities to meet good performers and people of high character. Each lesson with Klingler lasted about two hours, and Suzuki was given a rather long assignment of several compositions on which to work, in addition to the technical exercises. For Suzuki, it seemed very difficult, perhaps because he hadn't learned quite how to practice yet. The experience taught him the real essence of the musical art, and this is what he wanted to learn. He wanted to understand the art of music, and he was not at that time trying to be a concert violinist.

For the first four years, they worked mainly on concertos and sonatas. In the second four years they studied chamber music. Klingler had been a student of Joseph Joachim, and at times he had been a substitute for the violist in the Joachim Quartet. Following this experience, he formed the Klingler Quartet, and, of course, it was this group that brought Suzuki to such a fine teacher. So now Suzuki was doing what he wanted to do, studying the art of music with a teacher that had great artistic insight.

While in Berlin, Suzuki stayed at the home of a widow and her elderly maid, both of whom were slightly deaf. For Suzuki, this was a blessing, because he felt he could practice with abandon and not bother them.

During one vacation period, Klingler invited Suzuki to visit him at his summer place, "Krumbke in der Altmark." The summer place was really a refurbished, 19th century Gothic castle, complete with moat. Suzuki was overwhelmed by the edifice, and after he walked across the bridge, wandered inside the gate, and entered the castle grounds, he was taken by surprise as a hand grabbed him by the shoulder. He found himself looking into the eyes of an armed guard. His heart beat rapidly, but a member of the Klingler household chanced to look out a window, recognized Suzuki, and quickly came to his rescue.

Dr. Michaelis and Dr. Einstein

He also had a friend in Berlin, Dr. Michaelis, a professor of medicine, who was very kind to him. At one time, Dr. Michaelis had been in Japan and had been in the Suzuki home quite often. Suzuki had not been in Berlin too long when Dr. Michaelis received an invitation to become Dean at Johns Hopkins University. While Dr. Michaelis was staying in America, and being concerned for Suzuki's welfare, he asked a friend to look after Suzuki. The friend, as it turned out, was Dr. Albert Einstein.

Prior to his leaving for America, Dr. Michaelis gave a dinner party and he asked Shinichi to perform. He chose the Bruch *Concerto* which he was studying with Klingler, and after the performance, an elderly lady said to Dr. Einstein, "Suzuki grew up in Japan in a completely different environment from ours. In spite of that, his performance clearly expressed to me the Germanness of Bruch." Dr. Einstein, who was young enough to be the son of the lady, replied, "People are all the same, Madam." This experience had a tremendous impact on Suzuki.

Like Einstein, Dr. Michaelis was a fine musician. He used to accompany his wife, who had studied voice at the Vienna Academy of Music. Not only did he accompany well, but he could transpose at sight at the request of the singer. Once at a home concert, his wife was not feeling well, so she asked him to "play half a

Albert Einstein, also a violinist, presented this sketch to his friend Suzuki, dated November 1926.

step lower." Suzuki was astonished as he realized that not only was he transposing down a half step, but that he was doing so without the music. Suzuki later learned that Dr. Michaelis, like Dr. Albert Schweitzer, had great difficulty making a choice between a profession of music and one of medicine.

Einstein's musicianship was well known. His violin was his constant companion. He played Bach especially well and his fingers seemed to move so easily. Michaelis and Einstein really showed Suzuki what the study of music can do for a person, though they did not speak to him directly about it.

One of Suzuki's most unforgettable experiences occurred at an evening of music at the Einsteins'. On this occasion, an 18 year old boy, who was studying composition at the music academy, was asked to improvise. Einstein went to the piano and played a short theme. Then young Kaufman took the theme and said, "I will begin with an early composer. Here is a fugue in the style of Bach," and he proceeded to improvise. After this display, he went on to use the same theme and improvise in the style of Chopin, Beethoven, Brahms, Johann Strauss, and Mahler. This was Suzuki's first experience with improvisation and he was greatly impressed.

Einstein's circle of friends included many people of prominence in their particular fields of endeavor, but they all shared a love of art, and all were extremely modest and kind. Here Suzuki learned that in order to achieve harmony, one must be able to compromise gracefully. He also learned that it is nobler to be the one who yields than the one who forces the other to compromise. Harmony cannot be achieved in any other way. This, then, was the great attribute of character that Suzuki learned from Einstein and his friends. It would later become the basis of Talent Education. Suzuki's aim is to develop young Japanese children, who will grow to be fine adults, who can enjoy their music together, and who will develop as high an intellect and sensitivity as possible. The purpose of Talent Education is not to train professional musicians, but to train fine musicians, and then through music, the student will show a high ability in whatever field he might choose.

Einstein was only 16 when the idea of relativity first occurred to him. Einstein said that he discovered it by intuition, and that music was a driving force behind intuition. Einstein's parents began his study of the violin when he was six years old, and Einstein himself has said, "My new discovery is the result of musical perception."[5] It was an exhilarating experience for Suzuki to associate with people of such high intellect, sensitivity, and good will.

During the time when Suzuki was with Einstein, the scientist would frequently take Suzuki to concerts, and one of Einstein's good friends was the concert violinist, Adolph Busch. The scientist had great regard for Busch, both as a musician and as a person. "Before Busch's concert, Einstein telephoned to tell me what time to meet him at the bus stop. I was careful to get to the stop on time, but the eminent scholar was there before me. Even though I was a mere stripling, he had invited me as his guest, and treated me accordingly. I just bowed, and did not know what to do."[6]

---

[5]*Ibid.*, p. 90.
[6]*Ibid.*, p. 88.

Chapter 3

Waltraud

(1920-1928)

In Berlin

Many people in Berlin had concerts in their homes and provided their own entertainment and, of course, through Einstein and Michaelis, Suzuki was invited to other German homes. Here he came in contact with the world's great artists. One evening he attended a piano recital at the home of Dr. Franke and there he met his future wife, Waltraud Prange.

Waltraud, a beautiful, blond, 17 year old German girl, was attending that particular concert alone because her mother could not come with her, and when it was time to leave, Suzuki asked permission to take her home. She agreed, and on the way home, he said that he would like to meet her family. She told him her father was deceased, but he was welcome to come meet her mother, brother and sister. Suzuki, wasting no time, went the very next day.

It was the first time the Pranges had met a Japanese. Since all of the family were musical, they performed an evening concert for him. It was here that Suzuki found family life and love through music. The brother was a violinist, the sister and Waltraud both played piano, and Waltraud sang. At the time Waltraud

In a home environment filled with music, Waltraud frequently sang with her sister, a pianist, and her brother, an accomplished violinist.

was studying piano at the Stern'sche Conservatory, and she was the soprano soloist at her church in Berlin. Suzuki's brother, Fumiyo, was studying 'cello in Leipzig at the time and he, too, visited at the Pranges. Waltraud's brother had formed a band in order to earn money for the family and on evenings when he was working, Shinichi would play violin in the family recitals.

To better understand the works that he was performing, Shinichi decided to study composition, and since Fumiyo was in Leipzig, Shinichi chose to commute to Leipzig where he could study with Georg Schumann. With a twinkle in his eye, Suzuki recalls that after just three weeks of composition lessons, he attended a symphony concert where he heard a Brahms Symphony. Completely overwhelmed by the work, Suzuki went to Schumann and told him he could never be a composer. However, he told Schumann that he liked him very much as a person and wished to study with him. "Could I study orchestration instead?" he asked, and it was agreed. (This study is apparent in the charming duet parts, which he has written for portions of the first three violin books.)

During this era, a concert performer had to give a debut concert in Berlin to be accepted throughout the world, so all of the great musicians were playing in Berlin. Shinichi and Waltraud attended many memorable concerts, and they remember Kreisler performing; Glazunov conducting; Celia Hansen, a fine woman violinist; Richard Strauss conducting; a special concert where Mascagni conducted a chorus of 1000; Busoni's tender touch at the piano; and Furtwängler and the Berlin Philharmonic. They particularly remember the series which included the entire Beethoven Sonatas for Piano performed by Artur Schnabel.

Waltraud's brother, Alli Prange, performed professionally as director of his own small entertainment group.

Also at this time, without telling her, Shinichi was attending services at the Catholic church where Waltraud was soloist. One day he mentioned to her that he had especially enjoyed her singing and that was the first time that she was aware that he had been there. It was a very happy time in his life and he was adapting to Western ideas, but then he received a message from his father asking him to return to Japan. It was a tearful parting for both of them. Though Suzuki returned to Japan, Fumiyo remained in Leipzig and occasionally visited the Pranges.

The Marquis Tokugawa was now back in Japan and Suzuki was giving concerts there. But he was very depressed, and no one knew why. Finally he told his father that he wished to marry Waltraud, and shortly thereafter, he sent a telegram telling her that he would be returning to Germany.

Suzuki's father sent Umeo, the oldest brother, to Germany to meet the family and give his approval, and thus Shinichi and Waltraud became engaged.

After considerable "red tape," the wedding was set. The Prange family was half smiling and half sad. Smiling because of Waltraud's happiness, and sad because she would be leaving for such an unknown country. Shinichi said it would be better for them to live in Switzerland than in Japan, but Waltraud said she did not understand. If he had lived in Japan, it must be all right.

An Elegant Wedding

On February 8, 1928, the wedding took place, and is was like one would imagine in a fairy tale. After his return to Germany, Shinichi had studied Catholicism and became a member of the Catholic Church, so the wedding took place in the church where Waltraud had been soloist.

Shinichi Suzuki in a photograph designated Nagoya, 1926, about two years before his marriage to Waltraud Prange.

It was customary to use a wedding coach, and the Suzuki's coach was black with an off-white interior, pulled by two horses, and attended by two coachmen attired in off-white livery with black trousers and high top hats, one in front and one standing behind the coach. A red carpet stretched from the altar, along the aisle, down the steps of the church, and out to the coach. The wedding was absolutely beautiful with bells ringing and the pipe organ playing. As they walked down the aisle together, though, they did hear whispers of "a Japanese." The choir sang, and when they left the altar, a member of the choir played a violin solo, the *Ave Maria*, which was, of course, very important earlier in Suzuki's life. As they left the church, the bells were ringing to announce the wedding. The church was filled with friends, and many people had gathered to watch the bride and groom.

For the next four months they lived in Berlin, and then a cable came from Suzuki's father stating that his mother was seriously ill and they must return as soon as possible. When they left for Japan, Shinichi told Waltraud's mother, "Don't worry, we will come back every five years," but providence had different plans for the Suzukis. They did not live in Switzerland nor did they return to Germany. But perhaps if they had, Talent Education would not have been born.

To Japan by Train

They travelled to Japan by train via Siberia because it was more rapid than by ship. Arrival in Nagoya was extremely frightening to Waltraud. She could not speak a word of Japanese and there were no foreign newspapers or foreign radio stations at that time. Her only contact with the outside world was through Shinichi. Even her music was not available to her. She could not vocalize because of the thin-walled structure of the Jap-

Shinichi Suzuki and Waltraud Prange were married in Berlin, Germany, on February 8, 1928.

anese house and she had no piano. This was a very traumatic period in her life.

She came, of course, to a very beautiful Japanese house where there were many servants and chauffered limosines. The senior Suzukis lived well in this period of their lives, and while Shinichi was in Germany, his father had received the Second Order from the Emperor. When the Marquis Tokugawa was in Nagoya, they visited him at the famous Nagoya castle. After about six months, Waltraud's *Bechstein* piano, which had been a gift from her mother, arrived by sea. Once again she could express herself through music. She was learning to speak and life was much easier for her.

Not long after that event there was great sadness in the elder Suzuki's household. Before a year had elapsed, Shinichi's mother died.

Chapter 4

Out of the Ashes of Depression and War

(1929-1945)

The Suzuki Quartet

Shinichi concertized as a violin soloist and in 1929 a family string quartet was organized. The quartet consisted of Shinichi and his three younger brothers. They concertized extensively throughout Japan and became quite well-known in their homeland. He laughs when he tells of the first radio broadcast given in Japan by the Suzuki Quartet. The violist was the most emotional one; in climaxes he would rise up off his chair. When he did this during the broadcast the announcer thought he wanted his chair removed, and obliged. When violist Suzuki went to sit down again, he fell to the floor and the broadcast came to an abrupt halt. The announcer's explanation over the radio: "Machine Kaput."[1]

To supplement his income, Suzuki began to teach violin privately. His first young pupil was Toshiya Eto, who was four years old. Then came another infant pupil, Koji Toyoda. Koji's father lived in Hamamatsu. In the early part of 1930, the Suzukis moved to Tokyo, and soon after that Mr. Toyoda also moved to Tokyo with

---

[1]Clifford Cook, *Suzuki Education in Action* (Exposition Press, 1970), p. 76.

his family so that little Koji again came to Suzuki for violin lessons.

During this time the life of Masakichi Suzuki was changed by world events. With the crash of the stock market on Black Tuesday of 1929, the elder Suzuki was ruined financially. At one time the family owned a great deal of real estate and a considerable amount of property, but it had to be sold parcel by parcel and piece by piece to meet financial obligations. No one was aware of these difficulties because the chauffered limosine still arrived in front of the house. Masakichi made the statement: 'I will be responsible for every one. After all, the company, my property too, was all built through the effort and cooperation of my workers. I will not dismiss a single person as long as there is anything left. I owe it to them.'[2] Eventually even the Suzuki mansion had to be sold. Finally those workers, for whose future Masakichi wished to make some provision, had to be let go. With the working force decreased, the remaining ones moved to a smaller factory. To those people who had known the factory in former times, its successor must have seemed shabby and poor. To Masakichi, the object of an enterprise was not only to make money, but it was also a way of putting his high principles of life into action. The fact that the factory flourished again after the war can be ascribed only to the heritage, honesty and sincerity left by Masakichi.

During this time when all assets of Masakichi were being liquidated, he made a trip to Toyko to ask Shinichi to sell his *Vuillaume* violin, but this sacrifice was not enough for the young couple. He came again to ask Waltraud to sell her *Bechstein* piano. This was a sad moment for Waltraud because it was a gift from her family. It was even sadder because this meant that now she would be deprived of her music. But, she thought,

---

2*Nurtured*, p. 69.

The Suzuki String Quartet consisted of four brothers: Shinichi, first violin; Fumiyo, cello; Akira, viola; Kikuo, second violin. (Circa 1929)

"If I asked Shinichi to do something for my family and he refused, how would I feel?" So she agreed. They never had a fine piano again, because they could not afford one comparable to the *Bechstein*.

In 1930 the family business formed an aggregate, and after this, Masakichi was invited regularly by the Emperor to attend the garden festivals in Tokyo in the spring and autumn.

Suzuki's Teaching Attracts Attention

The early 1930s were a difficult period financially for the young couple. Suzuki still gave lessons to the young pupils that he had started, Koji and Toshiya. More and more young students came to their house for lessons, and it was a very exciting time in this respect. Suzuki

40   SUZUKI: THE MAN

took the greatest pleasure and delight in giving lessons to children, and they all became his friends.

> Koji first played on the stage when Suzuki's pupils gave a recital performance at the Nihon Seinenkan in Tokyo. Toshiya Eto was seven years old and that evening he played the Seitz *Concerto No. 3,* accompanied by the Tokyo String Orchestra. Yoko Arimatsu, just five, also played very well and after she finished, she shouldered her violin and ran off the stage. She was a charming little girl and we all burst out laughing. And, his sixteenth size violin under his arm, three year old Koji came to the stage. He played *Humoresque* while his father accompanied him on the guitar. The following day there were big photographs of Koji in the main newspapers and articles with the headings, "A genius appears," "Brilliant," "Wonderful," etc. Previous to the performance, I had told journalists: talent is not inherent or inborn, but trained and educated. Genius is an honorific name given to those who are brought up and trained to high ability. I had put emphasis on this and had repeated it.[3]

He was disappointed that they had not understood.

At this time Suzuki began to develop some of the basic tenets of Talent Education. One of the most important assertions was that any child can be trained and there is only one way. He set out to prove this with the brilliant achievements of the children in those early classes.

Toshiya at 11 received the first prize in a newspaper music contest sponsored by the Ministry of Education. The required composition was Bach's *A minor Concerto.* Little Koji, who was then seven, could play the same piece beautifully. Suzuki wanted the judging committee to understand clearly that even a Japanese who was only seven years old could reach that level and pass the test, and so he asked them to let Koji play, even though he was younger than the required age.

---

[3]*Nurtured,* p. 31.

Sightless Teiichi Tanaka was one of Suzuki's earliest Talent Education students, the first of many handicapped children to find success through the Mother Tongue Method.

"Gentlemen," he said, "I beg you to listen to Koji Toyoda play this concerto. You need not score him." So, at seven, Koji had already been brought up and trained to reach the level of the Bach *A minor Concerto.*

In 1937, Suzuki received two appointments to teach violin. One was at the Imperial Music School in Tokyo, and the other, at the Kunitachi Music School. These appointments greatly improved his financial situation.

Among those very first young students was Teiichi Tanaka, a boy of five who was sightless. He had lost his eyes from an eye disease when he was a baby. The father, who was an artist, brought the child to Suzuki saying, "My wife and I want to give our son a light in his darkness, a light that will shine throughout his life. We were thinking of music, and I came to ask you to accept him as one of your violin students."[4]

Suzuki realized that for Teiichi to play he must develop a different kind of "sense of sight," a sixth sense, or *Kan*. Together they set about to develop this *Kan,* and soon he was able to play as well as the other students. In 1942 when Suzuki presented his very young students in concert for the first time, some 30 children preformed at the Hibiya Hall. Along with Yoko Arimatsu, Koji Toyoda, Takeshi Kobayashi, and Kenji Kobayashi, little Teiichi performed a Seitz *Concerto.*

The War Intensifies

By 1943, World War II was rapidly changing the life in Japan. The Germany army had surrendered at Stalingrad, and in the Pacific the tide of conquest had turned. The Japanese armies withdrew from Guadalcanal, and life was very hard in Japan. The violin factory, which had been moved to Obu, had been reduced in size by the bombing. In 1941, Umeo, the oldest brother, had become head of the factory. The Nagoya factory had been converted for making seaplane floats, but there was difficulty obtaining an adequate supply of essential Japanese cyprus wood. Even though they wanted desperately to work, they could not. Someone needed to go into the Kiso-Fukushima mountains and obtain the cyprus. Suzuki visited his father to tell him about the situation and to ask him how to get permission to enter the forest. He also knew that as long as he stayed in Tokyo, most of his students would refuse to be evacuated, even though the air raids were getting worse. Suzuki informed both of the music schools of his plans to go into the forest.

As the bombings intensified, Waltraud urged Shinichi to leave Tokyo and move to Hakone. They had

---

[4]*Nurtured*, p. 56.

rented a small cottage near there at Lake Ashi that had been used for fishing. Because she refused to leave him and go alone, he finally agreed to go with her. Nevertheless, circumstances separated them. To obtain the lumber from the forest for the Nagoya factory, Shinichi had to move to Kiso-Fukushima. But Waltraud, who was a German, was not allowed to accompany him. All foreigners were looked upon with suspicion, and the fact that she was not a Japanese subject, even though Germany and Japan were allied, made no difference. Life for her was extremely difficult and unpleasant.

During the war, the Germans in Japan were evacuated to the mountain resorts of Karuizawa and Hakone. Since the Suzukis had a cottage at Hakone, Waltraud agreed to go there even though she would be alone. Food was extremely scarce, but in Hakone she was able at least to draw German rations, which, in part, included bread instead of rice. So, reluctantly, they parted for the duration of the war, hoping it would not last too long. Waltraud was harassed by the police a great deal. Alternately they accused her of being a spy and then insisted that she should be a spy for Japan. She had almost no freedom of movement and although she could not leave the "German village" to visit Shinichi, he could visit her from time to time. He vividly remembers that she gave him a precious apple that she had saved for him from her rations. In fact, he felt that it was too precious to enjoy himself, so without telling her, he took it to his sister's children in Kiso-Fukushima.

Shinichi went to live alone in the mountains, took over a *geta* (wood clog) factory, and converted it into a lumber yard to supply the float factory. Though he knew little about the lumber mill, he was able to get first class timber in the forest, and send it to Nagoya. The work went smoothly, and the manufacturing of the floats began to make good progress. Suzuki lived by the ideal that he would live as best he could whatever happened, and he would do whatever work he had to do. A Zen priest named Dogan had taught him this when he was young, so he was able to throw himself into the work at hand and gain from it.

Though the lumber mill work was interesting, the distribution of food came to a standstill as the war's effects became worse. Kiso-Fukushima is a town in a valley in the upper reaches of the river Kiso, and because the town is surrounded by mountains and small valleys, no food is produced there. During the final stages of the war, there was no distribution of rations at all. Since the factory was a war factory, it was possible to obtain things on the black market, but Shinichi positively did not want to buy on the black market. Adding to Shinichi's concerns was the arrival of his younger sister with her two small children. She had lost her husband and by coming to live with Shinichi, the short supply of food was strained even further.

> On factory holidays, we all went to the heart of the mountain to look for *warabi* (bracken), but with nothing to eat, other people had already picked it all. We then went along the mountain stream and found some water algae on a rock. It had a tinge of redness and a stalk. We stuffed our rucksacks to the brim with this and carried it home. We put it in a big pot of water, added salt and let it boil. The pot seemed to overflow with the stuff, but after boiling, there remained only a half bowl full. This, unlike mere drinking water, gave us some feeling that we had eaten gruel. In this manner we frequently kept off the hunger. It must have been bitter for my sister, not being able to feed her children. But the kindness and goodness of the people in Fukushima locality will be remembered all my life.

> We stayed with a family named Doke which included an old man. They all helped us warm-heartedly. If they managed to get good things to eat, we were always called. After such a treat, the house would come to life again.[5]

---

[5]*Nurtured*, p. 35.

Umeo, the oldest Suzuki brother, inherited the violin factory and is shown here with his son who now owns the Nagoya business. They are standing in front of a statue of Masakichi Suzuki, father and grandfather respectively.

The consequences of the war became more and more harsh. Then on January 31, 1944, Masakichi died at the age of 86. Without formal training he had turned out fine machine-made instruments. He continued with his own studies and his research until his death. In his lifetime he had acquired 21 patents. From childhood, Shinichi had learned countless things from his father, both morally and materially. Besides his ceaseless search and study, he taught him sincerity through the manner in which he lived.

At the factory in Kiso-Fukushima everyone worked with a great intensity. Feeling a responsibility for the workers, Suzuki tried to elevate their spirits by playing his violin for them each morning in the clear mountain air.

Finally the war ended.

Koji Toyoda Comes to Live

About this time, Suzuki heard that Koji's parents had died one soon after the other. Hurriedly he sent a letter to the old address in Tokyo. There was no answer, so he asked a friend in Tokyo where Koji and his younger brother had moved. After all, Koji's father had moved to Tokyo because of Suzuki, and with both parents gone, he felt that he could not neglect the boy. Then he asked NHK (the Nippon Broadcasting Station) to broadcast a message on their missing person program: "Koji Toyoda, I am in Kiso-Fukushima. Please let me know where you are."[6] After about two months, he received a letter with the name Toyoda on the return address. The letter was from Koji's uncle who had been taking care of him. Suzuki was so excited that he wrote him at once, and soon after, Koji, now 11, came to Kiso-Fukushima with his uncle. It had been three years since they had seen each other.

---

[6]*Nutured,* p. 36.

Koji's uncle had run a small *sake* drinking place in Hamamatsu. "Far from playing the violin, he helped me daily in the shop," said the uncle.[7] The uncle begged Suzuki to take care of Koji and then went home. From that day on Koji was a member of the Suzuki family and Suzuki's sister and her children were glad that Koji came to live with them.

Suzuki's sister gave Koji a great deal of motherly love as she raised him with her own children. Koji enjoyed life in Kiso-Fukushima. The family in the little valley now numbered seven. There was Suzuki's aunt with her girl helper; his sister, Hina, with her two children, Yasuo and Mitsuo; Koji and Suzuki. Every night they did something pleasant such as making up *haiku* and reading them. Though the poetry probably wasn't very good, the pastime was fun.

The time Koji had spent with his uncle in the environment of the *sake* bar had completely changed his behavior. They noticed an undesirable attitude and they began to scold and grumble, but it did no good. One day while Koji was away at school, Shinichi talked with the rest of the family and they decided they must create a new environment for Koji. Shinichi reasoned that if everyone displayed better manners and conduct in their daily life that Koji would eventually change. So they all changed their daily life toward a better attitude and good manners. What was originally planned for Koji turned out to be beneficial for all of them. It improved their minds and their own personal conduct. Within two years, Koji had mellowed into their way of life and the lifestyle of the *sake* bar had left no traces. He became a well mannered child.

So with the ending of the war, Shinichi was forming a new attitude about the education of young children. The beginning of Talent Education had started.

---

[7]*Nurtured*, p. 36.

Chapter 5

The Move to Matsumoto-Shi
(1945-1948)

Talent Education Is Established

The Talent Education movement was begun formally in 1945. Mrs. Tamiki Mori, a singer who had taught with Suzuki at the Imperial Music School, had evacuated to Matsumoto. Among the more culturally-minded people in Matsumoto, there was talk of founding a music school. Mrs. Mori was interested in the proposed school, and she sent Suzuki a message to Kiso-Fukushima asking him to come and help her. In reply, he sent her the following message:

> I am not very interested in doing "repair" work on people who can play already. I did enough of that before in Tokyo. What I want to try is infant education. I have worked out a new method I want to teach small children— not to turn out geniuses, but through violin playing to extend the child's ability. I have been doing research for many years. That is why I want to put all my efforts into this kind of education in the future. If my idea finds approval, I will help with the teaching along these lines.[1]

Suzuki soon received their answer. They consented to

---

[1] *Nurtured;* p. 38.

Dr. Suzuki enjoys a warm relationship with his sister-in-law, Shizuko Suzuki, pianist, who married his brother Akira. She has assisted him in the Talent Education movement.

his terms and wanted to help. At first, Suzuki commuted once a week between Matsumoto and Kiso-Fukushima. By the end of 1945 he decided to move to Matsumoto, and to start Talent Education at the Matsumoto Music School.

Though the war was over, Japan was an impoverished nation. People's money was frozen, and the amount of money allotted was so small, it was difficult even to buy food. When Waltraud was finally allowed to come to Matsumoto to see Shinichi, she had to stand on a crowded, smoky train for the nine hour trip. She felt extremely fortunate, however, because, quite by chance, she had gotten a job with the American Red Cross in Yokohama where the occupation forces had set up headquarters. Though Shinichi did not like the idea of her working, or of their continued separation, they had no choice under the circumstances.

Illness Then Insight

Since those early days when Shinichi became ill with
fever while working in his father's factory, he had had a
sensitive stomach; and by the end of the war his condition
was less than satisfactory. He rented a room in Asama, a
suburb of Matsumoto, and went there to recuperate. To
cook for himself seemed a bother and a nuisance, so he
soon neglected his own health even more. To prepare a
meal for himself, he would make a pot full of soup and
put an *o-mochi* (rice dumpling) in it to cook. He would
then eat this. For the next meal, he would put another
dumpling in what was left of the broth. He continued
this way for three meals a day until his health became very
poor. Finally, in desperation, he sent for his sister, Hina,
who was still in Kiso-Fukushima. Hina tried to care for
Suzuki, but when his wife, Waltraud, saw his condition on
her next visit, she was very upset, and immediately wanted
to stay with him. But Hina promised to stay and look after
him, and begged Waltraud to go on working for the Red
Cross because she was the only one earning money, and
without this they would all starve to death. Waltraud was
reluctant to return to Yokohama, but insisted that she
visit whenever possible, even though the journey sapped
much of her energy and time.

Suzuki's condition was diagnosed as a case of atony
of the stomach. The symptoms include a violent pain
caused by the inactive digestion, combined with a loss of
perception. One cold day, without knowing it, he crawled
out from under the *Kotatsu* (foot and hand warming
brazier of charcoal, set under a low table and covered by
a large quilt), and went to the corner of the room, put his
head against the wall and groaned. Hina was shocked and
frightened, but didn't know what to do. After a long
period of confinement in bed, Shinichi, weakened to the
point where he could no longer get up at all. Finally a
Miss Misake Koike, a teacher of piano at the Matsumoto

Music School, came to visit him. Shocked by the serious-
ness of his condition, she hastily summoned Mrs. Uehara,
a doctor of Chinese medicine. "The weakness and extreme
debility cannot continue," Mrs. Uehara pronounced.
"Ten more days, and it would have been too late. However, it is only the stomach and intestines; otherwise, there
is nothing wrong with him. . . . All right, I will begin my
treatment right away."[2] Mrs. Uehara prescribed steamed
and unpolished rice, and pickled vegetables. Though it
was an unusual diet, Suzuki believed in Mrs. Uehara's
rough treatment, and followed it, since his alternative
was death. To his great surprise, this radical diet reacti-
vated his stomach. A week later he could stand up, and
in a month he was able to walk outside, though very
slowly. As a result of this cure, Suzuki was most grateful
to Mrs. Uehara.

> Once before when I was convalescing at Okitsu, I
> had made the acquaintance of the Marquis Tokugawa,
> and that had resulted in the big change in my life from a
> white-collar worker to the world of music. During this
> second period of convalescence I invented a new system
> of calculation, not only for multiplication but also for divi-
> sion, addition and subtraction. I thought, "If I get well
> again, this will be something I can apply in my Talent
> Education plan." The Hongo Elementary School experi-
> mented with my system of arithmetic more than ten years
> ago, and it is now part of the curriculum of many elemen-
> tary schools of Japan, including those of Aichi-Ken, after
> observation and approval by the Ministry of Education.[3]

After the family moved to Matsumoto, Koji became
acquainted with a Catholic father, and began to attend
church every Sunday. Before long he became a Catholic.
Suzuki's sister, Hina, who was very close to Koji, accompanied him, and she herself joined the church about a

---

2*Ibid.,* p. 66.
3*Ibid.,* pp. 66-67.

In a move to preserve the magnificent Matsumoto Castle, the city was spared air attack during World War 2. Today the castle is open for the public to freely roam in its ancient halls.

year later. Hina not only helped at the church, but she also helped Suzuki in Talent Education.

Hina felt that Koji might eventually become a priest, and Suzuki agreed that it was possible, because, for Koji, art and religion were the same thing. Suzuki was certain that Koji would be a musician, although he would not hinder him if he wanted to become a priest. When Koji was about 14, his tone was very beautiful, and he had developed a high musical sense. After Koji had played the Bach *Chaconne* very well, the following conversation with Suzuki took place:

> Today you should go to church and play there before Christ. If you play with all your heart and soul, he will listen.
>
> "Yes, I will go," said Koji, and he took his violin and went to church, just around the corner.
>
> After an hour he came back. "I played the Chaconne in church."
>
> "Good, how was it?"
>
> "There was no one present; I felt very good."
>
> "That's fine. Wherever and whenever you play, always think that Christ is listening to you, all right?" Koji's cheerful face became even brighter, and he answered, "Yes." Gentle, obedient Koji![4]

---

[4]*Ibid.*, p. 39.

Chapter 6

In Ten Years
Anything Is Possible

(1945-1955)

Business In Earnest

When at last Suzuki returned to teaching, it was under the auspices of the Matsumoto Music School. With one violin and five children, he began the Talent Education Movement. Until he could obtain more small instruments, he took one violin from house to house for all of the children to share.

Finally he prevailed upon his younger brother, Shiro, to help him. Shiro moved to Matsumoto and set up a small family-run violin factory expressly to make small violins for his brother's pupils. The seven members of Shiro's family were employed. Even though they could never compete with the output of the Nagoya factory, which by this time had reconverted to making violins, their instruments were in great demand because of their excellence. Hundreds of small Shiro Suzuki violins were later sent to America. (In 1970 Shiro closed the Matsumoto factory and returned to Tokyo to fulfill his own dream of making high quality full-sized instruments.)

The Matsumoto Music School building was originally a school for *Geisha*. The rooms were small and this created problems for Suzuki when he wanted his students

As Talent Education grew, the small violin factory of Shiro Suzuki found a world wide market for its quality products.

to play together. The little house in which he lived was not much better, and so in 1951 he purchased their present home on Asahi. Then he was able to have larger classes, and especially the *kenkyusei*[1] and other teachers' classes in his home. Because the house had only *tatami*[2] rooms, the sound of the violin was muffled. Of course Suzuki was dissatisfied.

Waltraud continued to work in Yokohama for four more years to finance the big room which they added to the front of their house. This room was to be his studio until the opening of their present Talent Education Institute building in 1967.

It was in 1950 that Dr. Masaaki Honda visited Matsumoto to learn more about Suzuki's philosophy, and to explore the possibilities of bringing his daughter, Yuko, to study with him. Suzuki asked three girls, each about 10 years of age, to play for Dr. Honda. The three, Hiroko Yamada, Yuko Oike, and Tomiko Shida, played the Vivaldi *G minor Concerto,* and Dr. Honda was greatly impressed. Koji Toyoda, then 16 years of age, played the Beethoven *Concerto.*

Summer Institutes, Graduations Initiated

In the summer of 1951, Suzuki had his first summer school, or summer institute, as we call them in the United States. It was held at Kirigama, and it lasted five days. This summer school has now grown to such an extent that they have two sessions with a great many more students at each session.

Talent Education expanded rapidly in the 1950s, and branches were being established in the name of Suzuki that did not meet the standards of his original ideal. So the Board of Directors set up by-laws for the formation of

[1]*Kenkyusei* — student teachers.
[2]*Tatami* rooms are those with floors covered with rice mats.

Participants of all ages attended Suzuki's first summer school for Talent Education students. This annual event now hosts hundreds of students, and has fostered many similar activities in America.

new branches of Talent Education and recommended that the three following conditions must be met: (1) the branch must be recommended by a neighboring class; in other words, a class in an area that Suzuki had already approved must recommend the new branch for approval; (2) the new branch must have 25 charter members; (3) and the branch must be approved by the Board of Directors of the Matsumoto school. Thus, in the Shonan District, there were Talent Education programs in Fujisawa, Kamakura, Zushi, Odawara, and Mishima.

On October 25, 1952, at Kyoritsu Hall, the first student graduation was held. One hundred ninety-five students graduated, the hall was packed, and in the audience was Mr. Tokugawa, the man who had such an important part in Suzuki's career by taking him to Germany in the 1920s.

During this period, Koji Toyoda, the young boy who had come to live with Suzuki, was maturing both in stature and musical performance abilities. When Koji became 19 years of age, Suzuki realized it was time to select the best teacher for him, not only for his improvement as a performer, but also for his improvement as a person. They selected George Enesco, one of the 20th century's finest artists and most distinguished teachers.

*   *   *

I think it is important for their personality development that young people come in contact with distinguished persons. From my experience, I strongly feel that they absorb something of the heart, feeling, and deeds of such persons. Because of this belief, I selected teachers for Koji—Mitsuhiko Sekiya—and his wife, whom I esteemed. Mr. Sekiya is a professor at the International Christian University, and formerly taught at Shinshu University in Matsumoto. I begged Mr. Sekiya to take Koji into his family, and Mrs. Ayaka Sekiya, his wife, to teach him English so Koji could pass the test for going abroad to France to study. At the same time, I hoped Mr. Sekiya would be kind enough to teach him French. For Koji to have been with this couple of wonderful character for such a length of time is the most wonderful thing that could have happened to him. I, too, am grateful.[3]

In the fall of 1952, Koji left for Paris to study under the great artist, but in November, Suzuki received a letter from Koji with the following news: "I have passed the entrance examinations at the Paris Conservatory. Professor Benedetti is now my teacher. From a friend I heard the news that Professor Enesco was ill, and does not take on students."[4] Receiving this news, Suzuki was very upset He immediately wrote to Koji,

Didn't I want you to go abroad to study with Enesco? To hear only from a friend that Professor Enesco was ill and not to see for yourself, what kind of thing is that? You left Japan because I wanted you to study with this teacher. If you held the teacher in high regard, then you would not just listen to hearsay, but would naturally investigate for

---

3*Nurtured,* pp. 39-40.
4*Ibid.,* p. 42.

yourself, aside from whether or not you receive lessons. That is an entirely different matter.[5]

Shortly thereafter he got a message from Koji, saying,

> I received your letter, and I think I really matured on reading it. I looked up Professor Enesco's address and went at once to see him. I did meet him. He is a great and wonderful person. Advanced in years, and despite the fact that he felt a little weak he said, "Go ahead and play." Professor Enesco was so kind as to listen to me play the *Chaconne* by Bach. After I finished, the maestro said, "It is fine if you study with me here. But now you are a pupil of Benedetti and I cannot be so impolite as to take his student away. When you have graduated from the Paris Conservatory, you will be welcome." Professor, I will make every effort to graduate as quickly as I can.[6]

Suzuki sent the following letter to Koji:

Dear Koji:

> Thank you for your letter. . . . Wasn't it good that you visited Professor Enesco? You will one day realize that is the greatest and best blessing on earth to come in contact with men of high humanism, who also through their art have pure, noble souls. And whatever you can absorb of his greatness and beauty of character will determine your worth as a person. However, to perceive and grasp these qualities requires the humility and judgment that come only through sincerity, love and knowledge. That you can be close to Professor Enesco makes me, above all, to feel at ease, confident and happy. It is greedy of me, but I would like one more person close to you: Dr. Schweitzer. This really would be most wonderful. But however wonderful the other person might be, depends on us alone—whether we have the capacity to absorb their greatness. One has to educate oneself from within to benefit from the greatness of others. Only if one person can do this can one fully

---

5*Ibid.*, p. 42.
6*Ibid.*, pp. 42-43.

realize the joy of being near someone who is great. Never
lose your humility, for pride obscures the power to per-
ceive truth and greatness. Please, by all means, don't forget
this.[7]

Koji graduated from the Paris Conservatory in the
short time of six months. With great joy, he became the
student of George Enesco, and he studied with him for the
following two years until the master passed away. The
period with Enesco allowed Koji time to single out a
teacher for himself, and he chose Arthur Grumiaux, a
teacher at the Royal Music School in Brussels.

Sound Has Life and Soul Without Form

An event took place in 1953 which was to change
Suzuki's entire idea of tone and music.

One morning in 1953 a newspaperman telephoned
me to say that Jacques Thibaud was dead. . . . I was so
shocked that I was hardly able to coherently give the
reporter the impression of the great man that he sought
from me. I just stood there, holding the receiver. It was
like irreplaceably losing someone near and dear. After the
first shock the following thoughts came to me as I quietly
wept. I had never met Thibaud, but he had been living in
my heart for some time. I loved his playing and admired
him intensely. Having listened to his recordings for twenty-
odd years, I could sense his personality, and had been
studying his expression and way of playing. Music . . .
through sound Thibaud had come to life in my soul and
fostered in me   an ineradicable love and admiration.
Music . . . sound, tone. What strange things they are, I
realized at that moment. Man does not live in intellect.
Man lives in the wonderful life force. "Sound has life and
soul without form." That is when I thought of those words
that are now my motto.

---

[7]*Ibid.*, p. 43.

Fifty years ago, it was Tolstoy's "Conscience is the voice of God," and to live in conscience was my sacred creed. But now "conscience" has been changed to "life."[8]

Annual Concerts Begin

On October 25, 1953, the second graduation ceremony was held in Aoyama Gakuin University. Three hundred sixty-three children graduated this time, and afterward, it was suggested that the ceremony be held on a much broader scale, so that every child, whether they graduated or not, could both attend and play. So it was decided that in March, 1955, the First Annual Concert would be held in the Tokyo Gymnasium.

All of this transpired between 1945, when Suzuki moved to Matsumoto to set up his program, and the year 1955, when Waltraud returned to become a full-time wife. After 13 years of seeing each other only on week-ends and holidays, the Suzukis were reunited in their own home. Waltraud began to work very hard with Shinichi to promote Talent Education, both in Japan and in other parts of the world.

The house was soon filled with the sound of violins, voices, and the laughter of young students who went there to study. Several girls stayed with them, usually on weekends and holidays, because they were still in school during the week. Among them were Yukari Tate from Tokyo, Fumiyo Kaneko from Niigata, Etsuko Ohno from Yokkaichi, Naomi Ishida from Nagoya, and Yuko Honda from Fujisawa. These girls were like daughters to the Suzukis. This lively group came regularly, at least twice a month, except Yuko, who did not come as often as the others. The mothers of Yukari, Fumiyo, and Etsuko are still going to visit during the summer school, because they are very close friends of the Suzukis, even though their daughters are all married and now have children of their

---

[8]*Ibid.*, p. 95.

own. Occasionally, there were boys staying with them also, especially the Kobayashi brothers and, of course, Koji Toyoda, who spent his summers there.

During this time Suzuki worked diligently preparing his violin method. So important were the basics, that it took 10 years to complete Volume 1. In the first volume, there were several compositions which Suzuki wrote. Though he originally used Japanese folk melodies, he soon learned from teaching Koji and Toshiya Eto that the boys tired of the folk melodies, so he composed his own pieces for them. As the program grew, most of his former students from Tokyo heard of his whereabouts and came to Matsumoto to study.

In 1955, on March 30th, the First Annual Concert was held in the Tokyo Gymnasium. Over 1500 children participated, and members of the Royal Family were invited. Attending were the Crown Prince, Princess Chichibu, Prince and Princess Takamatsu, several grandchildren of the Emperor, plus members of several embassies and cultural centers from both in Tokyo and Yokohama. The concert was covered by the Japanese and foreign presses, as well as radio and television.

This is the first time that children came together from all over Japan, and they would perform without rehearsal. Knowing that children were used to following the piano, they placed speakers throughout the great floor of the gymnasium, so that all of the students could hear the piano and play together. The concert was a success that exceeded the expectations of those people involved.

The following article was written by Mr. Ragnar Smedslund, Consul General of Finland in Japan, after hearing the 1955 National concert:

> The scene is Tokyo's new Sportshall on a Sunday in March. The galleries are full of 10,000 spectators who, spellbound, are following the spectacle in the arena where 1200 violin playing children of the age of 4 to 15 are playing Vivaldi's Concerto in A-minor. In the middle of

the arena there is a platform with a grand piano and on all four sides thereof the youngest children are lined up.

The program was commenced by the first movement of the Mozart Violin Concerto in A Major, played by the 80 most advanced violinists. Thereupon, 120 of the next lower class joined them for playing the first movement of Bach's Concerto in A minor. And for each new item on the program a new group marched in until the total reached 1200. After the Vivaldi "Concerto" the program consisted of various selections of Bach, Lully and Handel.

Behind this concert there is an all-Japan organization for "the education of the children's talents." It has its headquarters in Matsumoto, Nagano Prefecture, and 65 branches in various parts of Japan. The total number of pupils is at present about 4,000. The founder and leader of this organization is a well-known violin teacher, Shinichi Suzuki, who naturally conducted this concert.

Everyone who was present at the concert in Tokyo Sportshall must have found it an eloquent testimony of the possibilities of bringing to light and developing children's talents at a tender age. And everyone of the audience is no doubt willing to subscribe to the statement by William James quoted in the program as follows:

> Compared with what we ought to be we are only half awake. We are making use of only a small part of our physical and mental resources. Stating the thing broadly the human individual lives far within his limits. He possesses powers of various sorts which he habitually fails to use.[9]

9*Suzuki Education*, p. 19.

Pablo Casals, the immortal cellist, was deeply touched and impressed by the Talent Education concert given for him in Japan. In the emotion-filled moments that followed, he expressed his congratulations to Suzuki and shared with the audience his faith in the power of music.

Chapter 7

We Amaze the World
(1961-1963)

Casals Pays A Visit

The 1960s were a very exciting time in the life of Suzuki, for one after another of the world's great musicians observed and applauded his work. The first and probably the greatest artist to appear in Japan in the 60s was Pablo Casals. At 10 o'clock in the morning, April 16, 1961, 400 children from age five to 12 stood on the stage of Tokyo's Bunkyo Hall with their violins ready to perform awaiting Casals with great expectation. As he entered he was greeted with enthusiastic applause from the parents and teachers in the Talent Education movement, and was greatly moved when he saw the children lined up on the stage. No sooner was he seated than they started playing a rhythmic variation on *Twinkle, Twinkle Little Star*. The maestro was visibly moved by what he heard. He listened to the performance intently and his emotion reached its peak when the children played the Vivaldi, *Concerto in A-minor* and then the Bach, *Concerto for Two Violins*.

Following this part of the concert, 15 young cello students taught by Yoshio Sato, a pupil of Casals, played Saint-Saens, *The Swan* and a Bach *Bourree*. To quote Suzuki:

When the children's performance was over, I went to Casals to thank him for having listened to them, but before I could finish, he threw both his arms around me and silently wept on my shoulder. How often I, myself, had wept at this beautiful, innocent outpouring of the children's inner life force! Now the 75-year-old maestro himself was speechless in this sublime moment before the sound of that life force. Mr. and Mrs. Casals went up on the stage, patting the heads of the children as they moved to the center of the stage. Chairs had been put there for them. Holding a bouquet of flowers the children had presented to them, they sat down. Surrounded by these sweet little Japanese children, and a voice shaking with emotion, the maestro spoke into the microphone.

> Ladies and gentlemen, I assist to one of the most moving scenes that one can see. What we are contemplating has much more importance than it seems. I don't think that in any country in the world we could feel such spirit of fraternity or cordiality in its utmost. I feel that in every moment that I have had the privilege of living in this country such proof of heart, of desire of a better world. And this is what has impressed me most in this country. The superlative desire of the highest things in life and how wonderful it is to see the grown-up people think of the smallest like this as to teach them to begin with noble feelings, with noble deeds. And one of this [sic], music. To train them to music to make them understand that music is not only sound to have to dance or to have a small pleasure, but such a high thing in life that perhaps it is the music that will save the world.
>
> Now, I not only congratulate you, the teachers, the grown-up people, but I want to say: my whole admiration, my whole respect and my heartiest congratulations. And another thing that I am happy to say at this moment is that Japan is a great people, and Japan is not only great with its deeds in industrial [sic], in science, in art, but Japan is, I would say, the heart of the heart, and this is what humanity needs first, first, first.[1]

---

[1]*Nurtured by Love,* pp. 114-115.

WE AMAZE THE WORLD 67

When Suzuki greeted Casals, he told him that he had been his pupil for a long time. Casals looked at him in surprise and said, "I do not know you." Then Suzuki, with a twinkle in his eyes, said, "I have been your pupil through your records which I listen to daily."[2]

> Pablo Casals deeply moved us with performances and he in turn weeps with emotion at the performances of the children that bring tears to so many eyes. This deep emotion in each · case is caused by the great and beautiful symphony of life in its purest state. The human heart, feeling, intellect, behavior and even the activity of the organs and nerves, all are but part of the life force. We must not forget that man is the embodiment of the life force and that it is the power of the life force that controls human seeking and finding. That is why Talent Education has to be an education that is directed to this life force.[3]

The second great musician to visit Talent Education in 1961 was Arthur Grumiaux.[4] At the invitation of the Osaka International festival, Grumiaux and his wife went to Japan and, of course, they went to Matsumoto where they met Suzuki for the first time. Suzuki was very impressed with Grumiaux's artistic ability, for by this time Grumiaux had been the teacher of Koji Toyoda, and later was to become the teacher of Tomiko Shida. Suzuki felt it was good fortune for his students to be working with such a person as Grumiaux, whom he felt was a good, warm hearted individual with a noble spirit, human kindness, simplicity, and naturalness.

2Personal interview by the author.
3*Nurtured by Love*, pp. 96-97.
4Arthur Grumiaux first played in public at the age of five. He received his musical education at the Conservatories of Charleroi and Brussels and later studied with Georges Enesco in Paris. It was through this tie of his having been a pupil of Enesco that Toyoda became Grumiaux's pupil after the death of Enesco. In 1949 Grumiaux succeeded his former teacher Alfred Dubois, as professor of violin at the Brussels Conservatory. Grumiaux has been one of the few great violin virtuosi of our time. Because of his many fine performances he was honored in 1973 with the title of Baron by the King of Belgium.

Increasing Recognition

During this time many articles were beginning to appear in American magazines extolling the merits of the Suzuki method. Among the visitors in the early 1960s was Professor N. H. Pronko of Wichita University in Kansas, who had been experimenting along the same lines as Suzuki, and found that babies brought up in different cultural environments during the first nine months were able to adapt themselves differently according to the environment. He published the results of his studies in the United States in psychological journals, and his finding corroborated the work of Suzuki. In his articles he made reference to the Suzuki method and stated, "Good environmental conditions and a fine education cannot help but bring children genuine welfare and happiness, as well as promising light and hope for the future of mankind."

In September of 1962, Suzuki received the following letter dated Berlin:

My Honored and Revered Teacher:
I have just come to Berlin. When you, Professor, were here, in which neighborhood did you live? I have always dreamed of seeing this place. All the new buildings in

Berlin seem somewhat cold. But the people differ from those of rural Cologne in elegance, refinement and politeness. Yesterday I was given an audition by the Berlin [Radio] Symphony Orchestra and appointed first concertmaster. The conductor—Fricsay—ranks at present in Germany with Karajan and Kubelick. The only worry I have now is whether I am really fit to take a position of First Violinist in such a famed orchestra.

With affection and most respectfully,

Koji[5]

This was an emotional experience for Suzuki, for this was the first time that a Japanese had won such a position in Europe. It was indeed a triumph for Suzuki and Talent Education.

The following year another Suzuki pupil was to bring great honor to her teacher. In 1963 Tomiko Shida won the International Music Contest in Munich. She stayed in Europe to become a pupil of Grumiaux and still resides in Brussels.

[5]Nurtured, pp. 29-30

Visitors to Matsumoto find abundant evidence of traditional Japan. Narrow, flower-adorned streets and alleys are adjacent to modern thoroughfares and architecture.

Chapter 8

Talent Education
Goes to America
(1952-1967)

Film Impresses Americans

Among those who attended the first graduation in 1952 was Mr. Kenji Mochizuki, who was to become a very important link for Suzuki to the outside world. Mochizuki had studied violin himself and played quite well. He became a student in the Oberlin Graduate School of Theology in Oberlin, Ohio and while there he was also a violinist in the College-Community String Festival Orchestra. Though he made tapes of that first graduation and took them to America, people were very skeptical. The Americans couldn't believe these were really tiny children playing together. Suzuki himself believed that if the American teachers were to support the Suzuki approach to learning, the Japanese teachers would then realize the importance of what they were doing and they would create additional support for the movement.

Mochizuki realized that the only way to impress the American teachers was to have a movie of the concert, and so the 1955 first annual concert was filmed.

> The film and tape were impressive. Huge numbers of Japanese children were playing from memory violin music ranging up to the level of the Vivaldi and Bach double

concertos. Aside from the sheer weight of numbers and the appeal of cute tots performing seriously, the outstanding features for the string specialists were these: (1) There was not a poor left-hand position or bow arm visible in the entire group. (2) Intonation was good and a pleasing tone was modulated expressively. In short, this was not just mass playing of 1200 children from five to thirteen years of age—it was *good violin playing*.[1]

Clifford Cook, who was an Oberlin Conservatory professor and also director of the orchestra, arranged for Mr. Mochizuki to show his film, to speak to his classes, and to appear before the Ohio String Teachers Association which met in May 1958. This appearance aroused considerable interest in the Japanese string movement.

Talent Education Is Outlined

Mr. Suzuki wrote after the Second National Assembly in 1956:

> If I had said ten years ago that I was going to have a group of over one thousand children, ages between five and thirteen, play Vivaldi's *Concerto* or Bach's *Double Concerto*, I don't think there would have been a single person in this world that would have believed me.
>
> Right after the war, when there were still many remains of destroyed buildings all over the city, I started this talent education. I started it because I realized how much these innocent children were suffering from the dreadful mistake made by the adults. These precious children had absolutely no part in the war and yet they were the ones suffering the most severely, not only in food, clothing and a home to live in, but also something that was very important, their education.
>
> I was teaching violin before the war and I found to my amazement that children show talent far beyond what their parents or the world expect of them. As long as they

---

[1]*Suzuki Education in Action*, p. 15.

Discipline and joy through violin playing is introduced at an early age in the Talent Education school while mothers remain close by.

have normal mental ability to learn, it has been proven that any child can be taught to play the violin.

However, there are two important factors. Young children have the natural ability to conform to atmosphere very easily. Therefore if we lose this period of life it is most difficult to teach the violin and get the same kind of result. Another important thing we must remember is that children learn by repetition. When we repeat one thing many times, this becomes a part of the child as his own talent. Watch the child learn his first word. His mother repeats the same word over and over to make him hear and learn it. But very soon these words will become a part of the child and this same child in a few years will be speaking the language so fluently that it may sometimes surprise his own parents or friends.

I applied this theory in teaching violin and taught to all my children Bach, Vivaldi, Handel and Mozart. Soon children learned to play many pieces by hearing the tune repeated many times and finally memorized the entire work.

Through this work the thousand children that gathered from all over the country were able to play together without having had any rehearsal. It is really not such a surprising thing.

We are not teaching these children to make them professional musicians. I believe sensitivity and love toward music or art are very important things to all people whether they are politicians, scientists, businessmen or laborers. They are the things that make our lives rich.

I am praying that the day will come when people all over the world will have truth, righteousness and beauty in their lives.[2]

---

[2]*Suzuki Education in Action,* pp. 16-7.

Though the film was made in 1956, it was not until the spring of 1958 that the Americans were to see it. The film itself was very difficult to obtain and the first print cost the Japanese 300,000 yen ($821.32). But even the second copy was to total 100,000 yen (approximately $275.00).

In the years between the 1955 Annual Concert and 1963 some American teachers visited Suzuki in Matsumoto. The first was Jacqueline Corina. Though her home was in California, her family was in Tokyo and so she was able to go to Matsumoto to study.

In 1959 John Kendall, then a professor at Muskingum College, New Concord, Ohio, made a short visit to Japan to learn more about the method. Also, he returned there in the spring of 1962 to attend the National Concert in Tokyo.

In the spring of 1963, Dr. Clifford Cook attended the ninth National Concert which was moved to Yokohama because of the extensive construction in Tokyo in preparation for the 1964 Olympics.

At this time preliminary arrangements began for the first group of Japanese children to tour the United States. The theme of the Fifth International Conference of ISME (International Society for Music Education) held in Tokyo in 1963 was the promotion of music education for all children around the world. Attending the Tokyo conference were Alex Zimmerman, then president of the Music Educators National Conference of the United States and Vanette Lawler, the MENC executive secretary, and all of the American delegates were well aware of the Suzuki program. The conference first heard the Suzuki-trained children in a massed group of approximately 500 children. They played at a special festival performance presented by Japanese students in which a combination of 6,000 children performed in choirs, orchestras and bands in the National Gymnasium in Tokyo.

The Tokyo meeting was the Fifth International Con-

Individual instruction at an early age with parental involvement is basic to Suzuki's teaching strategy.

ference of ISME and 512 persons were among the delegates representing 29 nationalities. In each country, except for the United States and Canada, the delegates are appointed by the National government and are, of course, financially sponsored by their government.

Among the important educators at the Tokyo ISME Conference was the Russian delegate, Dmitri Kabalevsky. Among the eleven delegates representing Germany was a Dr. Egon Kraus, who was the secretary-general of the ISME Conference and also head of the Music Educators for West Germany; the eminent teacher and orchestra director, Matti Rautio of the Sibelius Music Academy in Helsinki; and Dr. Elizabeth Szoenyi of Hungary representing Kodaly. The author was among the American delegates. In a recording that was obtained at that concert one can very well hear the excited voice of Kabelevsky as he shouted "bravo" at the end of the performance.

In July, 1963, at the International Society for Music Education conference in Tokyo, Suzuki presented proof of the success of his teaching philosophy through performance, and he reached many nations for the first time.

First United States Tour

Following the ISME Conference, those people involved in bringing the first group of Japanese children to the United States began to formulate a plan. The committee included Dr. Robert Klotman, president of the American String Teachers; John Kendall and Clifford Cook, who were among the first American string teachers to go to Japan, and Dr. Masaaki Honda. Financing was one of the most difficult problems of this project. It is the Japanese custom that if you invite someone somewhere, you are going to pay for it, so, of course, the Japanese took it for granted that if Japanese children went to America, somebody in the United States would pay for this hospitality.

In the end, a letter had to be sent to Japan stating that there were no funds available for such a trip. Financing was then arranged by the Japanese, and they were able to raise additional funds through concerts they were to give in America. It was a difficult and arduous task to prepare that first tour group. They worked until practically the last day to get visas, to have the children excused from school, and to raise the necessary funds for such an undertaking.

The original tour group, which numbered some 19 people, included 10 students from ages five to 13, Dr. and Mrs. Suzuki, and Dr. Suzuki's sister-in-law, Mrs. Shizuko Suzuki, who had helped him develop the piano method. Also with the group were Mr. Machiro Hirose, one of Suzuki's fine young teachers, and Dr. Honda, who was invaluable in two ways, as a pediatrician and as a translator for Dr. Suzuki. In addition, four Japanese mothers joined the group.

Children chosen for the tour came from Nagano and Aichi prefectures, and Tokyo. Matsumoto is in Nagano prefecture, Suzuki's home area of Nagoya is in the Aichi prefecture, and Mr. Hirose was a teacher in the Tokyo area. They were picked for the tour not only for their ability to play, but even more so on their ability to be away from home and miss school for a two week period. The highly competitive examinations of the Japanese universities make intense preparatory schooling most important and some Japanese are reluctant to miss even one day of school.

The trip for the children, scheduled for a March 5th departure, was not approved by the Japanese government until February 18. The children on that first tour included: Asako Hata, age 7; Chiharu Tamura, age 6; Keiko Fukuda, age 6; Yasuko Ohtani, age 7; Hitome Kasuya, age 6; Ruyugo Hayano, age 10; Fumiyo Kaneko, age 12; Yukari Tate, age 13; Isako Fukazawa, age 6; and Yoshibumi Kawana, age 8.

Suzuki had intended to rehearse the children enroute, but there was no time for this. As a result, they played their early performances without a rehearsal. Originally the plane was to land at Anchorage. However, a few days before the departure date, the airline changed their routing and this made their first stop in the United States in Seattle. Seattle was probably better informed about Suzuki than any other West Coast area because in January of that year, 1964, John Kendall had given a workshop at the University of Washington. Also, on that same January weekend, this author gave a workshop on the Suzuki method at the University of Oregon. Seattle drew people from the states of Washington and Oregon primarily because they had seen the 1955 film and had attended workshops just three months earlier. Also a nucleus program had begun at the Holy Name's School in Seattle.

Concert Without Rehearsal

The group arrived shortly after noon and their concert was scheduled for 3 p.m. at the University of Washington. There was no time for the Japanese to rest, and with no rehearsal, they were whisked away from the airport for the concert. What the audience did not know was that some of the tour children had not even met each other yet, much less had they played together.

Yet they were thrust on the stage to perform. The afternoon concert was rather informal, and included a question and answer period with Dr. Suzuki. Suzuki also showed some of the games the children played, and some of the things they did to improve their performance. The evening program was a formal concert. Imagine, these children had left Japan at 5:50 p.m. on March 4th, Seattle time, and arrived in Seattle on March 5th at 1:30 p.m. with a concert scheduled immediately that afternoon, and a second one scheduled that evening!

Though Suzuki felt that the first session was more of a rehearsal than a performance, let me assure the reader that as a member of the audience, the author found it a moving performance. To hear the tone produced by these

The first tour of Suzuki violinists from Japan to America (March 1964) literally stunned music educators. Pictured with the ten children are Dr. Suzuki and Kenji Mochizuki, the former Oberlin student whose desire to spread Suzuki's educational principles of "love" and "service" so greatly assisted the movement.

young children was a thrilling experience. At both performances, the children received a standing ovation. The American teachers wanted to ask Suzuki many questions, but there was little time for them at this initial concert-workshop. The concerts did lay the groundwork for workshops which he was to hold in the United States the following year.

Following the Seattle stop, they went to Chicago; next to the University of Southern Illinois where John Kendall was now a member of the faculty; to Boston and the New England Conservatory; and then to the United Nations, where they presented a concert in the Dag Hammerskjold Auditorium. Before leaving New York they played at the Juilliard School.

Concert for the
Music Educators National Conference

On March 15, 1964, the concert for which they had originally been brought to the United States was presented in the Grand Ballroom of the Sheraton Hotel in Philadelphia for the national convention of the Music Educators National Conference. This ballroom, which seats 5,000, was packed with people standing in the stairwells and every available place. John Kendall gave the following address to Dr. Suzuki:

There are moments in history when a place, a time, a man, and an idea converge to produce results of great significance. Such an historical moment occurred when Shinichi Suzuki began his experiments in violin teaching in Japan. The results have attracted widespread attention and have generated much speculation about the nature of musical learning and the way in which every human being develops in the early formative years. It is not that any particular segment of Suzuki's ideas is new, but rather he has thrown a clear light on the question we all wish to explore, how the human being becomes musical. Suzuki's ideas have struck fire in America because they go directly to the heart of a process universally intriguing: how infant human beings emerge from early shapelessness to the phenominal powers of the formative years. In the understanding of this process, as Suzuki points out, lies the future of the human race. It would seem that we have only begun to recognize the learning capacities of very young children. It is likely that teachers and parents who seek an easy way will be disappointed. However, those who have the energy, the imagination and the courage to experiment, to change and to grow with the teaching process will certainly find stimulation in the ideas of Suzuki. In a decade the stimulation of his ideas has moved violin teaching and performing to the forefront of educational experiment and study—a move that can only result in profound and positive influence on both. Countless teachers, parents and students in all parts of America are already illustrating that Suzuki's ideas bear fruit in our country as well as Japan. The relevancy of Suzuki's ideas may be demonstrated best through the constant work and expert teaching of dedicated people and it is appropriate that his faith lies ultimately in the great ability of human beings to improve themselves and their way of life. In addition to the success of his teaching methods—a success so dramatically demonstrated by his own pupils—we owe a debt to Shinichi Suzuki for his wide and significant contribution to the human condition.

The next hour of performance must have certainly been a highlight in the musical life of everyone who was in the auditorium that day. The first child was so small that an additional riser was built on the stage so she could be seen. The step to that platform was so high that Suzuki lifted her up to that level. Her violin was so small that you would think no one could hear her and yet as she played, the tone was not only sensitive and musical, but filled the hall. As the concert progressed, the audience became more and more astonished at the development of these young children, and when Yukari Tate played the Chauson *Poeme* to end the concert, the audience rose as one for a standing ovation.

In the March 25th issue of *Newsweek* magazine, the following article was written about the concert of the Japanese children in America:

> Seven-year-old Asako Hata playfully dropped a chunk of ice down her neighbor's back, and the long table of children at lunch one day last week burst into delighted giggles. Forty minutes later, Asako was standing on the stage of New York's august Juilliard School of Music, bobbing her head shyly to acknowledge the thunderous clapping that greeted her performance of a complicated Veracini sonata. The solo climaxed a concert that was at once impressive and absurd, in which ten tiny Japanese children, ranging in age 5 to 14 played Bach and Vivaldi that drew bravos from a highly critical audience of Juilliard students and faculty. If their applause was tinged

with sentimentaliy (when the children's teacher, Professor Shinichi Suzuki, stepped on stage to tune a 5-year-old's quarter-size violin, the audience sighed), it was nonetheless wholly deserved. "This is amazing," said Juilliard violin professor, Ivan Galamian. "They show remarkable training, a wonderful feeling for the rhythm and flow of music."

Playing without a conductor and using no score, the youngsters were a living testimonial to the validity of Suzuki's unorthodox teaching method. He starts his children about 3, but the first lessons are for the child's mother. She comes once a week with her youngster, and after three months has normally progressed to "Twinkle, twinkle, little star." "By that time," Suzuki explains in a mixture of German and English as expressive as his face, "the child has watched the mother play and wants to imitate her." Only then is the pupil given a pint-size violin. Through exposure to classical recordings and constant repetition, the child is ready to tackle simple Bach gavottes

Suzuki's influence, having spread throughout Japan and the world, is exhibited in traditional welcoming concerts for visitors from distant places, such as this group assembled to play for Americans near Kyoto in 1977.

within a year. The 150,000 children Suzuki's system has trained in 30 years are far from robots. They combine virtuosity with feeling so successfuly that when Pablo Casals heard a Suzuki recital in Tokyo, he rushed to the stage, shouting "bravo," and hugged the children.[3]

(Copyright 1964, *Newsweek, Inc.*)

If the American string teachers and musicians were astonished at the work of the young Japanese children, you can imagine what a thrill it must have been for Dr. Suzuki as a culmination of his many years of labor to promote such a program. The tour must have been extremely exhilarating for him and he must have gone home with a whole new world opening for him and his Talent Education method.

Coming to the United States had mixed blessings for Suzuki. Overwhelmed by the performance of the Japanese children, America's leading string pedagogues wrote glowingly of Suzuki's accomplishment, and thousands of teachers were quick to initiate programs bearing his name. Some of these early programs flourished under the direction of conscientious teachers who continuously sought to improve their teaching methods.

Unfortunately, most teachers grossly misjudged the depth of understanding necessary to implement a successful mother tongue program. Many struck out on their own, only to declare months later that they had abandoned "rote teaching."

Even those who attended Suzuki workshops found the instructional format less than adequate to aid them in a step by step approach to the achievements of Japan's teachers. Of course, the language barrier and cultural differences amplified the problems.

String teachers serving in the public schools eagerly embraced the notion that Suzuki students were apparently trained in groups, since their appearances gave that mis-

---

[3]*Nurtured by Love,* p. 117. Copyright *Newsweek, Inc.* March 25, 1964.

taken impression. However, the less obvious necessities of the successful method eluded most. Missing were the essential elements of the live performing model to emulate, the stress on posture and tone development, the intensive listening, and the basic philosophy under which the Mother Tongue Approach functions.

Consequently, within a short period of time, Suzuki's name had been blemished and one heard more and more negative things about the Suzuki method. This was very disturbing to Suzuki. Those people, who were interested and realized the importance of the Talent Education movement invited Suzuki to conduct workshops and help them develop programs in the United States. So from 1965-1969, Suzuki spent a major portion of each summer in the United States giving workshops on college campuses. His first workshop in 1965 was at the University of Washington in Seattle.

After the initial concert in 1964 on the Seattle campus, Mr. Villem Sokol, who was head of the violin department, asked Dr. Honda if there were a Japanese student who might like to come to the University of Washington to get a graduate degree and also teach the Suzuki method. Dr. Honda immediately thought of and suggested his daughter for the position. So Yuko Honda came in the fall of 1964 and spent one year there. She also worked with Sister Anella at the Holy Name's Academy. When Suzuki came to the workshop in the summer of 1965, Yuko was his interpreter. She also followed him to the workshops at Southern Illinois University with John Kendall and at Oberlin College in Ohio with Clifford Cook.

Workshops Become Popular

When word spread around the United States that Suzuki was giving workshops at various universities, then, of course, many people wanted to bring him to their

In many ways, students around the world share almost identical traits as they cope with the violin, playing posture, and their own responses.

university. During this time, Mr. Mochizuki, the young theological student at Oberlin, had attended a party at the home of Heinrich Roth, prominent string instrument dealer. Among the guests at that party was Sheldon Soffer, a concert manager from New York City. Mrs. Roth convinced Mr. Soffer of the importance of another tour of Suzuki-trained children, and it was from this connection that Soffer became the agent for Talent Education tours and for Mr. Suzuki's workshops in the United States.

In the summer of 1966, the Eastman School of Music, Rochester, New York, had a workshop of greater length, two weeks, which reached many of those people who are now very active in the Suzuki movement. The workshop was headed by Dr. Donald Shetler, who had been at Western Reserve University in Cleveland, Ohio. Dr. Shetler had attended the programs that took place in Oberlin and was a most enthusiastic follower. He was able to obtain funds from the New York State Council for the Arts to promote what was to be called "Project Super." Super being an achronym for *SU*zuki, *P*enfield, *E*astman, and *R*ochester. The Eastman School awarded full scholarships to 50 string teachers, one from each state, for the initial two week institute in July.

With the announcement of its grant, the New York State Council of Arts stated:

> The Eastman School of Music and University of Rochester, with Council support, will conduct a study with a controlled student population of about one hundred school children from the Rochester and Penfield public schools and the preparatory department of Eastman, to determine whether the Suzuki approach can be applied to the American youngster. The New York Council of Arts has applied to the National Council of the Arts for more support. Project Super in its initial studies will seek the answers to these specific questions: (1) Can the Suzuki approach, so successful in Japan, be adapted to the social and educational systems of the United States?, (2) Can string teachers with a variety of training and experience manage the approach with a minimum of training under Mr. Suzuki's direction?, (3) Is it possible that the pedagogical strategy of the approach might provide new developmental approaches to the teaching of other instruments or even other subjects?, (4) Will in-service sessions and evaluations of teaching carried out under Mr. Suzuki's direction during the project serve to indicate improved teaching and learning relationships?, (5) Can the Suzuki approach be used in a variety of school systems and in ·

communities of different socio-economic levels with equal success?, (6) Can private lesson-group lesson plans be programmed into the elementary school's schedule?

As a part of this project, Dr. Suzuki was to return to the United States every six months to evaluate and to assist the furthering of his movement through Project Super. As a result, each trip to the United States, and frequently trips of which few people knew, always included a stay in Rochester. Heading the project as a string teacher was Anastasia Jempelis, an instructor in the preparatory department of Eastman School of Music.

In June of 1966, the New England Conservatory conferred the degree of Doctor of Music on Suzuki for his work in music education. Later he was to receive honorary degrees from the University of Louisville (Kentucky), and from the University of Rochester (Eastman School of Music).

The second tour of the children was scheduled in the fall of 1966. With the management of Soffer, they had a full month's schedule of concerts, with very few open dates. It was a difficult tour because the concerts were not scheduled systematically across the country, but instead, demanded that they fly from one side of the nation to the other, and back again. Several of the children from the first concert tour returned. Probably the most notable was Yukari Tate, this time performing the first movement of the Tchaikovsky *Concerto.*

It was during the 1966 workshops and tour that the American String Teachers Association decided to arrange a trip to Japan by American teachers. If the United States were the size of Japan, American teachers would have by now been saturated with the Suzuki movement, but since the United States is so large, and even though Suzuki had conducted workshops all over the country, there were still many areas that did not know anything about this method. So, Suzuki sent some of his young teachers to centers where they could aid in the development of the program.

By this time, several major music schools had become very interested in the Suzuki approach.

Matsumoto's Talent Education Building

After the triumphal trips across the United States in 1966, many more groups were clamoring to have the tour group come to their city in the fall of 1967. Before this, back in Matsumoto, Suzuki began construction on his own building for Talent Education. He had a lot which was just behind the *Shimin Kaikan*[4] of that city, but when the city realized what he wanted to build, they secured a lot just across from the auditorium which they felt would be more appropriate for such an institute. Only the skeleton of the building was built before their funds were exhausted, and for two years the building had no additions made to it. Now, with some of the money made on the tour, Suzuki had great hopes of opening this building in the fall of 1967. In addition, while on each tour, he had been selling some of his *Shikishi* paintings[5] to help pay for the building. With this in mind, he invited the first group of American teachers to come to Japan to help dedicate this new building.

In the summer of 1967, Suzuki again toured the United States, doing workshops in cities across the country. He had left Matsumoto to begin the workshops in June, and he arrived home just one flight earlier than the Americans, so that he could be there to greet them when they arrived in his country. While in Dallas, the last city on the U.S. workshop tour, Suzuki confided to the author that six weeks earlier he had given Yukari Tate a lesson (Her lessons sometimes lasted for two days.). She had come from Tokyo, and at that lesson she had learned the first movement of the Brahms *Violin Concerto,* the Tar-

---

4*Shimin Kaikan* — city auditorium
5*Shikishi* — small silk-screen mounted on cardboard

tini *Devil's Trill,* and the Schubert *Sonatina.* He said, "I have been thinking. When we go home, how would it be, if on the first concert, I asked her to play the Brahms, and maybe on the second concert the Devil's Trill?" Much to the surprise of the author, he did as he said. Yukari played them without another lesson, and she gave excellent performances.

The tour for the American and Canadian teachers was exciting. The group was divided into three smaller groups. One group stayed in Tokyo, one went to Kyoto, and the third group went to Matsumoto. Each group had intensive study with teachers in their assigned areas for a five day period. Then all of the teachers went to Matsumoto to be present for the summer session. As the Western teachers travelled by train through Japan, they were treated to a train station platform concert in each city that had a Suzuki program. The concert was provided whether the train stopped at that particular station or not. In Matsumoto, the tour group observed the teaching of Suzuki-trained teachers from all over Japan. Approximately 500 children attended the summer school, and by the end of the week, all the American and Canadian teachers had made many friendships among the Japanese.

The culmination of the teachers' stay in Matsumoto was the dedication of the new Talent Education Institute.

Chapter 9

Dreams Materialize
(1967-1970)

New Building Is Dedicated

The opening of the new Institute building was an exciting event for the American participants. Together with the Japanese teachers, they formed an orchestra which would play for the dedication. All of the people who had worked to make the new building possible were on the stage of the *Shimin Kaikan,* just across the street from the new Talent Education Building. The new building, which had stood unfinished for two years for lack of funds, was ready to be opened. The anguish of getting the building ready for use was not over for Suzuki, however. At the last minute, those people who held financial notes against the building refused to allow him to open, even though the dedication of the building was going on across the street. When all looked hopeless, Mr. Masaru Ibuka, founder and chairman of the Sony Corporation, came to the rescue. Finally, the whole financial problem was solved by Mr. Ibuka. Suzuki's dream of a Talent Education center had finally materialized.

All of the financial problems that had delayed the use of the building had taken their toll on Suzuki. At the end of the dedication day he looked extremely tired, and many Americans were concerned about his health.

Shinichi Suzuki met the first American String Teachers Association tour group at the Tokyo airport, July 24, 1967. He greets author Evelyn Hermann and Margery V. Aber, Wisconsin, in the background.

After the American string teachers left Matsumoto, they took a short tour of Japan. While on this trip, on August 12th, at the Hotel New Osaka, the beginnings of Talent Education for the United States took a definite form. Previously, on March 26th, 1967, Suzuki, along with the late Dr. Howard Van Sickle, then president of the American String Teachers Association, Dr. Honda, who was International Chairman of the Board for Japan, John Kendall, Carl Schultz, and Kenji Mochizuki had signed a document entitled, "Some Steps Toward Organizational Plans for Talent Education in the United States." At the Hotel New Osaka, these minutes were read, and the 55 teachers, who were on the tour, sanctioned the beginning of Talent Education U.S.A., which was later to become the Suzuki Association of the Americas.

Most of the people present at that meeting were to become very active in the Suzuki Association of the Americas. Margery Aber, founder of the American Suzuki

Institute in Wisconsin, which is patterned after the summer school of Matsumoto; John Kendall, who was the first to bring Suzuki repertoire to the United States so that we might model the teaching method; William Starr, who has done much to further the teaching of Suzuki by making a series of television tapes and writing a book on the use of the Suzuki materials, *The Suzuki Violinist;* Jean Switzer and Dorothy Walker, both of whom are outstanding Suzuki teachers, and have been active on the Suzuki Association Boards; and, of course, the late Howard Van Sickle, who not only helped organize the original Talent Education Board of the United States, but who was also instrumental in taking American teachers to Japan for several summer sessions.

When the Americans left Tokyo, many Japanese students, teachers, and parents went to the airport to bid them good-bye. It was a tearful parting, because they did not know if they would see each other again. Suzuki must have felt well rewarded by their visit, because as they left he was now in his new office in the Talent Education Building, and he knew that the Suzuki movement was beginning in earnest in the United States.

To give the Suzuki movement in the United States more impetus, those American teachers who had been in Japan were clamoring to have the Talent Education tour group of children and Suzuki himself come to their cities. Suzuki by this time had reached his 70th year, yet he was just beginning his international projects. In Japan, the pace for Suzuki was demanding, but always he had rest periods during the day. He frequently refers to the pace as "Matsumoto time." When he came to the United States with the tours, he found that Americans were not satisfied with a couple of hours of his time in the morning, and a couple more in the afternoon. Instead they would plan to use every minute of his time and he would become exhausted. So the 1967 tour group went to the United States with Dr. Honda and some very fine, young Talent Educa-

In true Japanese tradition, the dedication of Suzuki's Talent Education Institute called for a lavish display of flowers and congratulatory messages.

tion teachers, but without Suzuki. Representing Suzuki was Mr. Hachiro Hirose, Mr. Mitsumasa Denda, Miss Yuko Mori, and Miss Yoshiko Nakajima. Yuko Hirose, wife of Hachiro Hirose, was the accompanist. Each of these teachers had graduated from Talent Education teacher training in Matsumoto, and were the finest examples of teachers in Japan. It was rewarding for Suzuki to know that the teachers he had trained in Japan could go as disciples of Talent Education throughout the world, expound on his philosophy, and the true meaning of Talent Education, as well as explain the technique which he used to teach violin.

When the American string teachers were in Japan, they had made friends with some of the Japanese teachers, and when these Japanese teachers came to the United States, they came, not as strangers, but as visitors to the homes of friends. This, too, is a part of Talent Education, because it builds strong, friendly relationships.

SOME STEPS TOWARDS AN ORGANIZATIONAL PLAN FOR TALENT EDUCATION IN THE UNITED STATES

Since its introduction in 1958-59, Talent Education has captured the imagination of teachers all over America. The growth of interest in the past five years has brought us to a second and crucial phase of Talent Education development. This growth necessitates some very careful organizational planning if the movement is to be established.

To protect Dr. Suzuki and the name of Talent Education in connection with various projects, grants and experiments, a project-making group in the United States is necessary.

In fact, the possibilities for foundation grants and government funding are greater than ever before, but can only be obtained or realized with careful preparation. Furthermore, the very multiplicity of the requests currently being submitted implies some central clearing house to avoid confusion.

An increasing number of teachers will wish to travel to Japan. Not all of these will be equally qualified for time and attention at the Talent Education centers in Japan. Some preliminary screening of applicants in the U.S. would be helpful.

The certification of teachers is basic to the success and sound growth of the movement. Dr. Suzuki, with the help of an advisory group, should carry out this project. The U.S. Board of Directors of the Talent Education organization in America should conduct teacher certification with the advise [sic] of Dr. Suzuki.

Because of the vast geographic areas involved, the diversity of persons interested and the tremendous need for these teaching methods, it is imperative that some organization be formed to deal with the development of Talent Education in the United States.

Dr. Shinichi Suzuki, Dr. Howard M. Van Sickle, Dr. Masaaki Honda, John D. Kendall, Carl Shultz, Kenji Mochizuki. March 26, 1967

In consultation with Suzuki, first steps were taken during the 1967 ASTA tour toward formation of a Talent Education organization for the United States.

Waltraud Is an Active Aid to Suzuki

During this period, Waltraud became Suzuki's strong right arm. Her job was to translate and to answer all foreign mail. She was very fluent in English, so it was an easy task to translate, but the amount of correspondence continued to increase until the job became unbearable. Besides, many of the correspondents, who were eager to get more information, had very little, if any, understanding of the philosophy.

Suzuki had written a book in Japanese, for parents to read, but the book was written in an erudite style. When the American teachers learned of the book, they immediately clamored for an English translation for the American parents. Several people were asked, but all said it would be too difficult to translate into English, because one had to be able to read thousands of Japanese and Chinese characters. In many cases, a character was not

Members of the First ASTA tour to Matsumoto gather on the front steps of the newly dedicated Talent Education Institute. Among the group behind the porch rail are Waltraud and Shinichi Suzuki, Japanese teachers Mitsumasa Denda and Hachiro Hirose, and Kenji Mochizuki of New York.

Shinichi Suzuki and Evelyn Hermann share their joy in the dedication of the new building and the visit of American teachers.

just a word, but a whole thought or idea. Realizing the importance of this book to people outside of Japan, Mrs. Suzuki was determined to make it available in English. With the help of Mrs. Masako Kobayashi, Mrs. Suzuki was able to understand the Japanese. Then she translated it into English, with the help of Mrs. D. Guyver Britton, whose husband was connected with the British Embassy in Tokyo. Waltraud had to look up almost every Japanese character in the dictionary, and then verify the meaning with Mrs. Kobayashi to be certain she had the correct translation. Once she understood the Japanese, she then had to translate it into English. (Since her mother tongue was German, she was working with two foreign languages.)

Mrs. Suzuki did not tell her husband that she was working on this translation, and several times he asked her what she was doing so late at night, but she avoided answering him. After many months of difficult and demanding work, the book was finished, and she was able to present it to her husband. Almost immediately the book was published in the United States under the title *Nurtured by Love*.

Without this translation, Talent Education could not have spread throughout the United States as effectively as it has. When parents read it, they instantly want the concepts to become a way of life for their children. When teachers read it they learn the importance of their life's work. *Nurtured By Love*, first edition, was available in the summer of 1969. In 1980, it was in its 16th printing, and is available also in German, French, Dutch, Finnish, and Swedish.

All these years Waltraud had worked side by side with Shinichi. She had helped him and his family after she went to Japan, and she continued to work away from home for many years. When she finally joined Shinichi in a house of their own in Matsumoto, he brought his students to the house for lessons. This continued from 1953 until the summer of 1967 at the opening of Talent Education Institute. When the Institute became a reality, there was still much demand on Waltraud's time for answering foreign mail. Only after their golden wedding anniversary in 1978 did she declare that she was in semi-retirement. Now, some of the foreign mail is answered by office personnel at the Institute.

Progress Has Been Made

As the decade of the 1960s came to a close, Suzuki saw the fulfillment of some of his goals. Talent Education in Japan was flourishing, and Talent Education in the United States was making good progress. There were dedicated teachers in certain pockets of Japan that truly understood his method, and. they themselves were producing some very fine young students. Some of his early students had come to the Western Hemisphere, and were, through their demonstrations and talks, deepening the American teachers' understanding of the philosophy of the Suzuki method.

Project Super at the Eastman School of Music had greatly helped the Suzuki movement, in part by merely endorsing Suzuki's work. It was the first major conservatory to have a complete Suzuki program. Other conservatories were a bit more skeptical of the new approach, and in those cases where there was an involved Suzuki teacher in a conservatory that itself did not condone the Suzuki program, that teacher would establish a Suzuki program outside of the environment of the school. Young Suzuki-trained students were flourishing, and the teachers with traditional European backgrounds could no longer deny the possibilities of great success with the Suzuki program.

One of the reasons Suzuki wanted to have the Talent Education Institute building in Matsumoto was to have a place available for foreign teachers to work and observe as they studied with him. Earlier, when he was teaching at his house, it was impossible to accommodate everyone. Now there was an auditorium where they could give concerts. His Japanese teachers had classrooms where the foreign teachers could observe. Teachers from outside Japan came to take the same teacher-training course that all of the Japanese Talent Education teachers were required to take. Suzuki had built a "better mousetrap," and people from everywhere wanted to learn how to be Talent Education teachers.

Before, he had to travel to other countries to show them how the Suzuki method worked, but now teachers from other countries were coming to him. Some of the world's greatest performers had seen and heard his children, such as Casals, Grumiaux, Kogan, and David Oistrakh. From the smallest child to the most famous performer, all were impressed with the genius of Shinichi Suzuki. One immediately feels the warmth of the person, and his great, outgoing personality. His love of children is very evident, no matter with whom, or where he is, and the child always comes first. Such is the love of Suzuki for children.

The Talent Education Institute viewed from the park filled with lilacs in front of the building.

Chapter 10

For the Happiness of All Children

(1970-1980)

Suzuki Continues Study and Growth

At an age when most people have retired, Suzuki was just getting his "second wind." But the Talent Education Institute was deeply in debt, and it seemed to be operating continually at a loss. Undaunted though, Suzuki continued to explore new horizons in the field of pedagogy. His attitude toward the debts was that what he was doing was for the children, and there had to be a way to pay for it. Somehow, someone would find the money for him.

Suzuki had not given up any of his old teaching obligations, but had only added to them. In the 1950s, when the first graduation was held, it was decided that a tape would be sent to Suzuki for each child who wished to graduate. He would listen to the tapes, and make a personal comment for each child. This system worked well in the 1950s. The first graduation had only 195 tapes. By the 1970s, he was listening to over 5,000 tapes, and this became an enormous task. He was rising at 3:30 AM to begin listening to tapes before he left for school, which was a little before 9:00 AM each day, and the task consumed a great deal of his time and energy.

One of the things he noted in listening to these tapes was that there was a wide variation in tempi and interpre-

In his eighty-second year, Shinichi Suzuki maintained an active teaching schedule.

tation, and he decided that a set of practice tapes should be developed. First, they made these practice tapes directly from the recordings that the children listened to prior to learning each composition. There were some problems with this however, because the artist's performance was accelerated sometimes in order to get· all of a composition on one side of a record. Sometimes compositions were played with a certain flair or interpretation which Suzuki felt needed to be changed for the sake of the children who were to model them. Then he had another problem. He discovered that some people were using tape recorders in which the speed varied, thus changing the pitch of the recording as much as a half step sharp or flat. He got the cassette recorder companies to develop new tape recorders, with variable speed, so that all recordings could be played at A=440 Hz. (standard pitch). The project of having tape recorders manufactured with a variable pitch took the major portion of the 1970s to accomplish.

There were other accomplishments however, and many of Suzuki's lifelong projects were now starting to take form. In 1970, the first group of American children went to Tokyo to perform at the Internationl Concert, and they also studied with Suzuki in Matsumoto for a week. The first group was small, only 15 people, but the experience was a revelation to them. They found a different Suzuki in Matsumoto. In the United States, he was a man in a foreign country, speaking a foreign language, and he was under constant pressure to hurry. At home he could proceed on "Matsumoto time," as he did with the Japanese children.

First European Tour

That same year, 1970, there was another first. The Japanese tour children made their first trip to Europe, although Suzuki did not go along. Instead, Dr. Honda, along with two other teachers, went with Mrs. Suzuki, who acted as interpreter. Their first stop was Berlin, Mrs. Suzuki's home town. It must have been quite an emotional experience for her to return to her home city with the young Japanese tour group. From Berlin they went to London, and then to Lisbon, before continuing to the United States.

American Suzuki Institute

During the summer of 1971, the first American summer camp was begun in the name of Suzuki, and was called the American Suzuki Institute. It was held on the campus of the University of Wisconsin at Stevens Point by Margery Aber, and children from all over the United States attended.

In 1976, 18 American Suzuki Institutes were held in various parts of the United States. The program had grown enormously. In the late 1960s, Talent Education USA became the national organization uniting the American Suzuki teachers, but there were also some Canadian teachers in the group, and so the title USA was not all-inclusive. In the summer of 1972, a meeting was held at Stevens Point, Wisconsin, during the camp session, and the name was changed to The Suzuki Association of the Americas. The organization became a firm backer of the Suzuki method in the United States. The first officers of the SAA were: president, William Starr from the University of Tennessee, in Knoxville; president-elect, John Kendall, University of Southern Illinois; vice president, Louise Behrend, Juilliard School; secretary, Elizabeth Mills, Altadena, California; treasurer, Milton Goldberg of Winnetka, Illinois. The editorial board of the newly named American Suzuki Journal included Clifford Cook, then at the Oberlin Conservatory; Alfred Garson, Montreal, Canada; Evelyn Hermann, Dallas, Texas; Anastasia Jempelis, Eastman School of Music; and Sanford Reuning, Ithaca, New York. Other board members in the organizing group were Margery Aber, Wisconsin and Diana Tillson, Connecticut. During the first two years, which were vital to the formation of the organization, Harriet Mogge acted in the capacity of executive secretary. (At that time Ms. Mogge was a member of the staff of Summy-Birchard, publishers of the Suzuki books in the United States.)

Shinichi Suzuki with members of the faculty of the American Suzuki Institute, Stevens Point, Wisconsin, are pictured in the summer of 1976 when he was first recipient of the "Suzuki Chair" established there. Distinguished visitor was Clifford Cook, in flowered shirt to Suzuki's right, now retired.

Through this decade, the Suzuki Association of the Americas contributed in several ways to the dynamic growth of the Suzuki movement. Not only did it establish requirements for institutes and workshops, and audition students for the special concerts, but it assisted with the protection of the name of Shinichi Suzuki. In addition, its help to Suzuki was instrumental in the establishment of the International Suzuki Association and the international workshops. Finally, the Association served as a model for other Suzuki organizations around the world, and these groups have now drafted their own charters.

Early Development Association

In 1971, through the Early Development Association, Suzuki and members of the EDA began a project to study environmental conditions and their influence on young people. Suzuki hoped to document many of his theories. With advertisement in the Tokyo newspaper, they asked for young women who were in their eighth month of pregnancy to come and meet with them, so that they might help these young mothers establish a controlled environment for their child from the day of birth. There were only two prerequisites for the women: (1) they must live close enough to the EDA building to commute, and (2) the expected child was to be their first. At this time, it is still too soon to measure the success of the program.

More Tours to Japan

In 1972, the second group of American children participated in the spring concert in Tokyo. This time the group was quite a bit larger than the 1970 group. A total of 55 people from all over the United States went to Japan. It was a grand concert, and members of the Japanese Royal Family were present. The American children were much more advanced musically, as compared to the first group, and Suzuki was very pleased when he heard

Average youngsters develop above average ability through education designed to utilize their full potential.

Members of the Japanese Royal Family attend an Annual Gradua-
tion and Grand Concert held in the Budokan, Tokyo. From left to
right are the Empress' sister-in-law, Empress Nagako, Mrs. Masaaki
Honda, Crown Prince Akihito and Princess Michiko.

them. He said, "Now it is good for us to hear what you are doing in the United States." The other Japanese teachers felt that the contact alerted their own students to the fact that all children around the world were learning by the Suzuki method, and many were playing as well as the Japanese children. That the children learned so much from playing together was probably the most exciting happening. They entered the halls not being able to carry on much of a conversation, because the only Japanese that most of them understood was *"Konnichi wa,"* but they soon were able to understand each other, and the American students went home with many gifts and many new Japanese friends with whom they continued to correspond.

The Empress of Japan was present at the 1972 concert in the *Budokan* in Tokyo. She had not seen one of these concerts before, and she is quoted as saying, "The most exciting part of this concert is seeing the American and Japanese children performing so beautifully together, and without special rehearsals. Music is truly international."

As has been noted before, in 1964 Robert Klotman, then president of the American String Teachers Association, had been the person to extend the invitation to Suzuki to bring a group of 10 children to the United States to perform for the Music Educators' National Conference to be held in Philadelphia. Now Robert Klotman, as president of the Music Educators National Conference, again asked Suzuki to come to the national meeting to be held in Anaheim, California. The American children who had learned by the Suzuki method during the intervening ten years, along with two of the youngest children on the 1964 tour, would perform at this concert. The tour group was the largest ever to go to Japan, a total of 77 people, including students, teachers, and parents. From that group of children, 25 were chosen to perform in Anaheim. The performance was impressive. Not only did the Japa-

Commemorating the tenth anniversary of his appearance at the Philadelphia MENC convention, Suzuki returned for the 1974 MENC meeting at Anaheim, California, bringing two of the girls, now 16, from that first tour. Hitomi Kasuya, left, performed the Beethoven "Concerto" and Isako Fukazawa the Tchaikowsky "Concerto."

nese girls, now 16 years of age, perform well, but the American children played well, also. One of the Japanese, Hitomi Hasuya, performed the first movement of Beethoven's *Violin Concerto,* and another student, Isako Fukazawa, performed the first movement of Tchaikovsky's *Violin Concerto.*

First International Suzuki Teachers' Conference

Suzuki, never satisfied with his achievements, is always looking ahead. In 1974, he was looking ahead to the first International Teachers' Conference, to be held at the Hawaii Hilton Village in Honolulu, during the last week of June, 1975. This would give him an opportunity to work with teachers from all over the world in master classes, and would allow him to have closer contact with those people who were leaders of the Suzuki movement in other countries. Approximately 700 people participated. The conference was a great success, with American and Japanese teachers performing. Suzuki was truly exhilarated by that week, and immediately following this conference, he wanted to plan for a conference again the following year. In the end, he was persuaded to wait for two years, in consideration of the travel costs for the participants. In 1977, the second International Conference was set again for Hawaii. This time the teachers from Australia and several European countries participated in the planning, and it was gratifying for Suzuki to meet with representatives of several countries in one big session, and his joy was increased because all were so eager to learn more, and to improve the work they were doing.

Special Birthday Celebration

In 1975, Suzuki celebrated his 77th birthday. In Japan that birthday is very special, but his "old" pupils were unable to be together in October for the celebration, so it was decided that a special concert should be planned for the following April. In the spring of 1976, five outstanding young men whom Suzuki had trained, and who are now concert artists, performed at a very special concert in Tokyo. The performers were: Koji Toyoda, Toshiya Eto, Kenji Kobayashi, Takeshi Kobayashi, and Takaya Urakawa.

It was an impressive performance for all that were present. The stage was a "sea of flowers." Mr. Eto said he did not realize how great his first teacher was, and that he was just beginning to understand the importance of the man.

Another speaker who added his congratulations was the Marquis Yoshichika Tokugawa, now in his eighties. This was the man who had been Suzuki's mentor, and had persuaded Suzuki's father to allow him to study the violin; the man who had taken Suzuki to Germany, and who backed him in every way possible when he returned to Japan by lending his name to Talent Education whenever he could; and the man who came to every important event that Suzuki had in Japan. The Marquis Tokugawa died shortly after the 77th birthday celebration, but all were glad that he lived to be a part of it.

At the end of the concert, Suzuki went to the stage to acknowledge the performers, and to speak a few words to the audience. When he played the "Nagoya Lullaby," the audience was moved to tears. It was a highly emotional experience for everyone.

More Workshops and Conferences

The summer of 1976 brought Suzuki to the United States for more workshops. It was the 10th anniversary of Project Super, which began at Eastman School of Music in 1966. He also conducted a workshop at the University of Wisconsin at Stevens Point, where the University endowed a chair in his honor. He was the first recipient of this chair.

At the Second International Conference in Hawaii, in 1977, the planning for the year 1978 took place. The events of 1978 were almost overwhelming. First of all, Suzuki was in his 80th year, a time when most people have long since laid down the reins of their career. In February, Shinichi and Waltraud had their Golden Wedding Anniversary. Because of the weather, and the difficulty with travelling to Matsumoto, it was decided to hold the celebration of the anniversary during the spring weekend of the Tokyo National Concerts.

Golden Wedding Anniversary

On March 18th, at the Grand Palace Hotel in Tokyo, a big celebration with over 600 guests took place. People

Among the respected violinists nurtured by Suzuki are Toshiya Eto, Takeshi Kobayashi, Koji Toyoda, Kenji Kobayashi and Takaya Urakawa.

who had not been together for many years converged on Tokyo to be a part of it. Many gifts were offered, but perhaps the one of greatest significance was the gift from the teachers to the Suzukis. As has been noted before, when the Suzukis first came to live in Tokyo, Mrs. Suzuki had been asked to give up her fine *Bechstein* piano, a family inheritance, in order to pay the salaries of the workers in her father-in-law's factory. Since that day, almost fifty years before, they had not had a good piano in their home. The gift from the teachers was a new *Yamaha* piano, which was to be built especially for them. The presentation was made by Mr. Masaru Ibuka, president of the Sony Corporation. Of course, the piano was not ready, so he substituted a toy piano. Mrs. Suzuki had not been on stage when the presentation was begun, so when she saw the toy piano, she exclaimed, "I do not want

The Marquis Yoshichika Tokugawa, an early influence on the events of Suzuki's life, attended the master teacher's 77th birthday celebration.

this. I want a real one." Then, much to her surprise, they told her the toy was in lieu of the real one that was being made, and would be delivered in May. On the day of the Golden Wedding Anniversary, Shinichi said to Waltraud, "The second fifty years will be easier."

More Dreams Are Realized

In the summer of 1977, a young American tycoon, who had read *Nurtured by Love,* and was impressed with what he had read, made a trip to Matsumoto to meet the master. In their conversation, he asked Suzuki what he had planned for the future. Suzuki told him of the environmental studies with the young mothers. He hoped to document the importance of environmental conditions for the young child. He also said that he would like a special building in which this research could be carried on, where teachers could be trained, and where young mothers could come to study. So David Smith of Atlanta, Georgia, proceeded to help Suzuki finance such a building, and told him that within a period of ten years it would be debt free. The second thing that Suzuki told David Smith was that he would like to have an international concert with equal number of American and Japanese children. So with the financial aid of Mr. Smith's company, International Horizons, 100 Japanese children were brought to America. Along with 100 American children, they gave performances in Kennedy Center in Washington, Symphony Hall in Atlanta, and Carnegie Hall in New York City. The concerts were well received, with standing ovations wherever they were given. In Kennedy Center, President Jimmy Carter came to the stage to congratulate Suzuki and the children. While in Washington, Suzuki had an opportunity to speak with the President, and tell him about his views of education from

Appreciative "students" of Suzuki honor him at his 77th birthday celebration. Congratulating Suzuki are, from left to right, Toshiya Eto, Takeshi Kobayashi, Koji Toyoda, Kenji Kobayashi and Takaya Urakawa.

zero years of age. This concert tour and his meeting with the President fulfilled another dream for Suzuki.

Immediately after returning home, a group of Japanese children performed for Rotary International, which was having an international conference in Tokyo. Suzuki had already been named a Paul Harris Fellow by the trustees of the Rotary Foundation of Rotary International. The citation read: "In appreciation of tangible and significant assistance given for the furtherance of better understanding and friendly relations between peoples of the world."

Among the other important awards which Suzuki had received during the 1970s was the Gold Medal of the

A radiant Suzuki in his 78th year belies his age in both appearance and energy.

The emotional intensity of Suzuki's performance at his anniversary celebration is transmitted to all listeners.

Third Order of the Rising Sun, presented by Emperor Hirohito. He had also received the Spectrum Award of the World Organization for Human Potential, and in 1972, he received his third honorary doctorate, this one from the University of Rochester at Eastman.[1]

During the summer school in Matsumoto, enough money was collected from families in the small remote village of Matsumoto to commission a Japanese artist to make a bust of Pablo Casals, and Suzuki's students performed for the dedication. It was a joy to know that, in this provincial area, people understood the importance of music, and erected a statue of a musician from a far distant country.

The Suzuki Method building was completed during the spring of 1978, and the children from the kindergarten

At their 50th Wedding Anniversary celebration, Mrs. Suzuki talks with Philip Scheldt, American teacher, while Dr. Suzuki holds one of two gold-bound copies of "Nurtured By Love" presented to them by Evelyn Hermann.

[1]For copies of the citations, refer to Chapter 11.

Mrs. Suzuki is at first skeptical about believing that the toy piano presented to her actually represents a real one to be delivered later.

Suzuki greets Marianne Klingler, daughter of his beloved teacher in Germany, Karl Klingler.

Housed in a new building which opened in 1978, the Suzuki Method Institute will further the development of the Mother Tongue approach in many areas of study. Above: the architect's model. Below: photos of the building.

In a rare public performance, Waltraud Suzuki provides a special treat for those attending the 50th Wedding Anniversary celebration.

Suzuki proudly presents the 200 children of the 1978 International Talent Education Tour to President Jimmy Carter and his wife Rosalyn on the stage of Kennedy Center, Washington, D.C. The Carters' daughter, Amy, was studying in the Suzuki method.

and some of the offices of Matsumoto Talent Education were moved into the new building. Now Suzuki had a headquarters for the study of the education of children from zero years of age.

In August of 1978, the Third International Suzuki Teachers Conference was held in San Francisco. It was a great success with Japanese and American teachers working together with American and Japanese children. After the conference in San Francisco, Suzuki went directly to the International Society for Music Education Conference in London, Ontario. There, 30 selected American children performed together over a period of three days to

A monument to Pablo Casals stands in the park in front of the Matsumoto Talent Education Institute, a gift to Suzuki from Japanese teachers.

World Organization of Suzuki Talent Education

鈴木才能教育研究会世界組織。

Purport.
   To study and develop the mother tongues method.
   To spread the idea and philosophy of Talent Education.
   To respect and develop potential of all children
   To increase friendship and understanding through
   out the world by music

母国語教育法を研究・発展普及させる
才能教育研究会の思想、秩序を世界に知らしめる
子供の可能が生を尊敬し伸ばる
音楽を通して世界の友情及び理解をふかめる。

Art. 1, Member consist of Suzuki Association of the
   - world.
      世界の鈴木才能教育のメンバーにより会員を構成する

Art. 2. Each Country represent three directors.
   Country who has over 100 members can have
   two extra members. Totaling five
      各国は3人の理事を選ぶ33但し会員100人以上
      の国は2名追加. 計5名とする.

Art. 3. Board of Directors will. select. one President
   and   vice Presidents
      理事会は会長1名. 副会長   名を選ぶ33.

Art. 4. Annual fee per member is   dollar.
   This include two tapes from Matsumoto
      年会費は 1名   ドルとする. これは松本より
      の 2本のテープ代を含む.

Art 5. World Conference will be held every year.
   世界大会は毎年開催する

Art 6. Head Office will be at Matsumoto Japan.
   本部は日本の松本に置く

P.S. Art. 23. Board of Directors select   executive
   Director. 理事会は連任理事   名を選出する

An outline of the World Organization of Suzuki Talent Education
as proposed during the Teacher's Convention in Munich, 1979.

demonstrate the work of Shinichi Suzuki. Again, it was a milestone, for it was in 1963, at the ISME Conference in Tokyo that the world learned first hand about the Suzuki movement. At this exciting meeting, Suzuki received many standing ovations, and was lauded as The Music Educator of the conference. He immediately began planning in earnest for the 1979 International Conference to be held in Munich, Germany.

What a year 1978 had been for this master musician! Any one of the big events which he had planned for the year would have been enough for a younger man, but he felt time was not to be wasted because of his age, so he put it all into one year, and it was a glorious one!

In 1972, Suzuki informed this author that he guessed that he would have to live to be 100, because he had so much he wanted to do. In 1974, he had already raised that number by 10 years, and said, "I must live to be 110, because I cannot get it all done in the years left to me." And each year he comes out with new, bigger, and better ideas for the "happiness of all children."

He is probably one of the most exciting pedagogues in the world. He never relaxes with a feeling that the best way of teaching a point has been developed. Shinichi Suzuki spends all of his waking hours looking for new ways to improve teaching methods for small children. It is truly a privilege to sit at the feet of such a fine educator and musician. In years to come, students who have had the opportunity of being in his presence will realize that Suzuki truly devoted his life to the betterment and happiness of children throughout the world. Former Oberlin professor, Clifford Cook, who was among the first Americans to teach the Suzuki method in the United States, stated, "What Suzuki has done for young children earns him a place among the benefactors of mankind, along with Schweitzer, Casals, and Tom Dooley."

Waltraud and Shinichi Suzuki pose for a photograph to commemorate their 50th Wedding Anniversary, 1928-1978.

Chapter 11

Awards

Shinichi Suzuki

Your concept of Talent Education as originally developed for the children of preschool age in your native land has proven to be one of the most revolutionary forward steps in music education of the twentieth century. From a modest beginning in Japan, when your country was still prostrated by the horrors of war, it has grown to a movement that now includes more than 120 teachers and 6,000 pupils. Many of these have risen to high artistic levels in the international world of music. Furthermore, by bringing your young students to our country, you have elicited wide admiration and approval in professional musical circles, and the methods of your Talent Education are proving to be as successful in our country, and indeed, our city, as they have in Japan. For bringing beauty into the lives of so many, we are proud to award you the degree of Doctor of Music (Honoris Causa).

Citation, Commencement 11 June 1967
University of Louisville

University of Louisville, Doctor of Music degree, awarded to Shinichi Suzuki, 1967.

Dr. and Mrs. Suzuki share pride in the display of his medal representing the Third Order of the Rising Sun presented to Suzuki by the Emperor Hirohito.

SHINICHI SUZUKI
Doctor of Music

Inspired teacher of children, whose vision and dedication have produced a renaissance in the playing of stringed instruments, we express our gratitude for all the happiness and joy you have given the world in the making of music, with this, our highest honor.

New England Conservatory of Music, Doctor of Music degree, awarded to Shinichi Suzuki, 1966.

University of Rochester
(Eastman School of Music)

In 1972, Suzuki received his third honorary doctorate from an American University. It was bestowed by the Eastman School of Music of the University of Rochester, an institution which had already exhibited great interest in Suzuki's work by supporting, with the assistance of grants, a series of workshops done by him personally over a period of three years beginning in 1966.

SHINICHI SUZUKI

Countless small children today on both sides of the broad Pacific know the joy of music, not through passive listening but through skillful performance with their own hands and hearts of the works of the masters. The faith and dedication of Shinichi Suzuki have brought about this revolution in the musical education of the young.

Born in Nagoya, Japan, Shinichi Suzuki was self-taught in music until, at the age of twenty-one, he began formal studies in Tokyo. In 1928, after further training in Berlin, he began a successful career as concert violinist and teacher in Japan. It was there, after the second World War, that he developed the movement that has been aptly called Talent Education for the Happiness of All Children. Beginning with Japanese children, the innocent victims of war, the movement spread to other lands and transformed the lives of thousands of children and their parents. Ever growing, it affords the thrill of real accomplishment and the spiritual and emotional nourishment of great music to all the children of the world.

February 12, 1972
UNIVERSITY OF ROCHESTER

Diplôme d' Honneur

décerné à

Shinichi Suzuki

par la

Fondation Eugène Ysaÿe

pour sa contribution au culte du souvenir et à la diffusion de l'œuvre créatrice du maître.

Bruxelles, le 5 septembre 1969.

Le président,

Dr. Shinichi Suzuki was honored on December 17, 1969, with a diploma presented to him by the Ambassador of Belgium on behalf of the Eugene Ysaye Foundation. The **Diplome d'Honneur** *cites him for his contribution to the promotion of Ysaye's memory and creative works. It is dated September 5, 1969.*

THE SECRETARY-GENERAL

21 May 1970

Dear Mr. Suzuki,

I am writing to tell you how much I enjoyed the concert given at the Festival Plaza by your children's orchestra on the occasion of United Nations Day at EXPO '70 on 13 April 1970. I can assure you that the performance of the children was one of the most spectacular and impressive shows I have ever seen.

I should like to take this opportunity to thank you heartily for being instrumental in giving the concert and contributing to making United Nations Day a very successful and memorable occasion.

Yours sincerely,

U Thant

Mr. Shinichi Suzuki
3-10-3, Fukashi
Matsumoto City, Japan

From the Secretary-General of the United Nations, U Thant, Suzuki received this letter of appreciation for the performance at EXPO '70 for United Nations Day, April 13, 1970, in Osaka, Japan.

THE WORLD ORGANIZATION

FOR HUMAN POTENTIAL

Acting in its role in
Accordance with the Fourth Objective
of Article I of the Constitution

Does herewith laud, honor and
in all ways demonstrate
its esteem for

SHINICHI SUZUKI

AND DEDICATES THIS 19TH DAY OF MAY, 1973, TO CONFERRING

UPON HIM THE

SPECTRUM AWARD

OF

THE WORLD ORGANIZATION FOR HUMAN POTENTIAL

More than a quarter of a century ago, Shinichi Suzuki experienced a startling revelation: very young children possessed extraordinary sensitivity. "Given opportunity to learn," he said, "small children could develop their abilities far beyond what anyone would expect of them."

Suzuki taught music and loved music--fine music.

He was aware that appreciation of fine music added a devine dimension to the human experience. He resolved to spend his life helping precious children gain that appreciation at a time in their lives when their astonishing sensitivity could be refined and honed and polished as never again in the future: during the very early years.

By example, by proving that his children learned and had their lives enriched, he struck a powerful blow against those pedagogues who had established harmful practices of delaying the introduction to music until after the ephemeral and acutely sensitive period of the early years had passed.

The Suzuki Method demonstrated--in the case of unthinking and hurtful comments by those who held opposing views--that the lives of children: and the adults they became; were indeed made fuller and more meaningful: that, indeed, the ineffable joy that attends achieved potential was brought measurably closer.

For his insight, his struggle, and his contribution,
SHINICHI SUZUKI is herewith decorated with . . .
The Spectrum Medal of The World Organization for Human Potential.

For Himself

For His Service

For His Nation

And

For People of Love the World Over

The Spectrum Medal of The World Organization for Human Potential was awarded in recognition of Suzuki's insight, struggle and contribution toward developing full potential by helping children gain an appreciation of music during the very early years; he "struck a powerful blow against those pedagogues who had established harmful practices of delaying the introduction to music until after the ephemeral and acutely sensitive period of the early years had passed." Bestowed May 19, 1973.

The Sixth Mobil Music Award

The *Japan Times* of Sunday, October 10, 1969, carried the announcement of Suzuki's selection as the recipient of the Sixth Mobil Music Award, Western Classical Music Division. It followed the recommendation of a panel of judges comprised of Keisei Sakka, Marcel Grilli, and Takeo Murata, and carries with it a Mobil trophy and monetary prize of 500,000 yen.

The *Times* article briefly outlined his background and named some of the violinists who studied with him and have become known internationally. It also states, "Today, more than 30,000 Japanese children and over 200,000 children abroad are learning to play the violin" through the teaching approach that he developed.

Editor's note: *Dr. Suzuki has received numerous commendations, citations and awards, of which a few outstanding ones are mentioned in this text and displayed if possible. It should be apparent by reading this book that his concern for the Talent Education movement, the welfare of all children, and harmony among nations precludes his keeping a detailed or even accurate record of temporal recognition. This certainly is not due to a lack of appreciation, but simply that other concerns seem more pressing. We invite the reader to share with us any documentation of other recognition of Suzuki that might be included in subsequent editions of this book.*

Shinichi Suzuki:
His Philosophy

International Society for Music Education
July 4, 1963
Tokyo, Japan

Special Session: Education in the Community

Every Child Can Become Rich in Musical Sense

by Shinichi Suzuki
Chairman of the Talent Education Society,
Matsumoto, Japan

It is a great pleasure to welcome you who have come so far to this small Oriental Island, of which even Columbus was unaware. I would like to take this opportunity to make a proposal and ask for your cooperation.

I would propose that you foster in each of your nations a movement that will cause every child to grow up as a richly musical person. This would be a blessing for all children and is not an impossible thing to realize. For I have found that every child is born with the capacity for becoming richly musical so long as he or she is brought up properly. This is something I have learned in the course of my thirty years of experience in this field.

Two facts that have become clear in these thirty years are: (1) if any child is brought up so that he hears good music (e.g. through records) every day from the time he is born, he will become a person with a rich musical sense; and (2) if any child is brought up so that he hears off-key, distorted music every day, the child will become tone-deaf.

Do not these findings tell us something important about the whole question of the hereditary transmission of human abilities and about the problem of poor environment? If a child could not be brought up to be tone-deaf, the universal belief that a talent for music is something certain children are born with would be merely an illusion. This has been my conclusion, and for many years I have held that there is no such thing as an innate aptitude for music. I believe the same, of course, about other cultural skills. I have insisted that it is a mistake to think that hereditary aptitudes exist for literature, mathematics, or any such specific cultural activity.

This whole question is a very important one, and one which I hope you will study. For if we are to create superior methods of education, we must first understand the human being and how human abilities start to grow.

How Ability Grows

Although we may assume that we know much about man, I feel that we actually know very little about the real facts of man. In the field of growth in ability, many problems are posed to which we must give new thought.

The fact that ability does not develop without experience, for example, leads us to think about organisms and their environment of that time. Hence, even though there may have been innate differences among individuals everyone remained at the Stone Age level in the development of their abilities.

However, the fact abilities develop in response to environment opens up educational possibilities without limit. This is an important fact, because it means that if a child born today were brought up in a society five thousand years more advanced than ours, it could grow up into a person with the abilities of people five thousand years in the future. My observations have led me to conclude that:

Ability develops as a function of the effort of the life force to maintain itself—to survive by adjusting itself to its environment. I believe that in the field of education we must not forget that ability does not grow where there is no experience.

What Are Innate Individual Differences?

When it is realized that great differences of ability between two individuals are the result of differences in environmental conditions and the ways in which they were brought up, the question arises as to what should be considered the factors determining innate individual differences.

My thinking on this point is that:

Differences in ability to respond to the environment constitute differences in innate ability. They may also be regarded as differeces in capability for survival. An organism that cannot respond to its environment will die. We could say that an individual who possesses the capacity to respond quicker and more sensitively than another to his environment is an innately superior being.

Fostering Musical Sense

In various parts of Japan today, there are members of our Association who are bringing up their babies on music, letting them listen every day to good music on record players.

A masterpiece by Bach, Mozart or Schubert, for example, is selected and the one selection is played every day for the baby. If the record is played every time the baby starts to cry, it will eventually reach the point where it will become quiet the moment the music begins and will listen attentively. Only the one selection must be used.

After about five months, any baby thus exposed will clearly learn the selection. There are some babies that have been brought up listening to a concerto (one movement only) by Bach or Vivaldi and have learned the music well. After about five months, another selection is added. The baby hears two selections every day. In this way, any baby will grow into a child with a rich musical sense. In other words, the environment develops a person's ability.

In order to produce a tone-deaf child, a record off-key, distorted music, could be made and played daily from the time the baby is born. Since there has been no family thus far that has requested such an experiment with their baby, we have not tested this idea. However, without carrying out such an experiment, we already know some parents who have been raising their babies by singing lullabies out of tune every day and have fostered tone-deaf children, thus providing evidence for our purpose.

The method described above has its parallel in the development of a child's ability in its own native language in every country in the world. In any country, there are delicate differences of language native to the locality, and every child acquires completely the subtle differences of intonation and pronunciation of its locality.

Life creates ability. And the type of education that focuses on the marvelous power of children to grow in ability is the best type of education.

Talent Education

The fact that children of every land develop into adults with a very fine ability to talk fluently in the language of their country is really an amazing result of education. Thirty years ago, it was a surprise to me to realize the significance of this fact.

It is an amazing fact that language education does produce excellent results in developing any child, that any child does grow into a person of such excellent ability in his language depending on the way he is trained.

The growth of ability in one's own native language shows us that any child will develop, depending on the kind of development program applied.

If a teacher finds a pupil whose ability has not been developed properly and assumes that the child's ability is inherently inferior, the teacher may do well to remember, for the sake of the child, that the pupil has the great capacity of speaking fluently his own difficult native tongue.

The development of ability in one's native language is, I believe, the best type of education in existence. It is in the conditions making up this kind of education that the best educational method can be found, for all children throughout the world have successfully grown up in this field of spoken language.

Talent education merely applies the method of learning one's native language to education in music or some other subject.

Education Through Living Situations

The first point to learn from the child's education in his native language is the fact, from very simple beginnings, each item is applied in daily living situations until he fully absorbs it. In my educational method this is a primary point to which I strictly adhere.

For example, when a child learns to play a selection A for the first time, I tell him: "Now you have learned to play a piece; so let's start lessons to play it very well." I have the child practice this piece every day until he absorbs it thoroughly. Then he starts on selection B, practicing both A and B. When A and B are fully mastered, a third selection C is added.

After A, B and C are fully mastered, another selection, D, is added. Selection A is practiced daily at home, while B, C and D are taught until they are fully mastered.

The idea is to add one new item at a time. Because training in one's native tongue takes place by this system, every child thoroughly absorbs the language. When the selections are learned so thoroughly that they are a part of the child, then the ability that has been fostered to this stage becomes a powerful capacity that can be applied to learning the next new selection. The child therefore does not feel it particularly difficult but readily develops both his ability and his playing of a new selection.

The record player is the teacher in the home. The selection is played on the record over and over again until the tune is learned well beforehand, and then the child is taught to play it.

The children are instructed to be able to play at any

time any of the many selections they have. This is the system of native language training. Children who have been taught in this manner from the beginning are able to perform easily.

The three important aspects of music education are (1) fostering musical sense, (2) developing performing ability, and (3) developing behavior and the mind (character). We keep these three aspects always in mind, placing emphasis on education in the home and developing the child in cooperation with the parents to become a good person.

For the Sake of All Children

When parents unwittingly raise their children to be tone-deaf in the home, or when children grow up without their ability being developed because their parents have done nothing about it, the music educator who has them put into his hands finds only a frustrating struggle to try to train them, for no matter how hard he may try, the children remain as the tragic products of mistaken upbringing. I am struck deeply by the misfortune of these children, all of whom were born with the wonderful capacity of showing the same type of ability as they show in their own native tongue.

I hope that an age will be created in our countries when babies are brought up listening to good music in every home, so that all children will be rich in musical sense. The cooperation of record firms will be needed.

This should be a primary national policy, in making music education succeed. Casals said: "MUSIC WILL SAVE THE WORLD." This will happen if we exert our efforts towards this end.

I am deeply grateful to be counted as one of those who know that music has been an invisible but mighty living power to save mankind.

Music Educators National Conference
March 1964
Philadelphia, Pennsylvania

Outline of
Talent Education Method

by Shinichi Suzuki
President of the Talent Education Institute in Japan

Most people seem to think, even now, that one may not become a successful musician unless he has musical talents. That is to say, they think all successful musicians have been born with musical talents. I cannot agree with this. This idea of mine started 27 or 28 years ago, and it was at that time that I started on Talent Education.

Mr. Toshiyo Eto, who is now teaching at the Curtis Academy of Music in Philadelphia, was my first child-pupil. His father brought him to me when Toshiyo was only 4 years old. It was my first experience in teaching such a young pupil and I was quite concerned about it. The thought that came to my mind at that time was in regard to a child's mother tongue. A child will learn to speak Japanese when he is born and reared in Japan. The normal child can use more than 3,000 words at the age of six. This would certainly indicate that the brain of a normal child is quite active. This is the same the world over. I thought at that time that this fact should be of great importance to mankind. We should always keep in mind that few children are born mentally deficient.

Now let us turn to the talent of a child. Do Japanese babies have an aptitude for Japanese as soon as they are born? No. If a Japanese baby is born in England or America and brought up by English-speaking parents, that baby will grow up and learn to speak English. The same is the case with any baby, regardless of national origin. That is to say—any child will learn any language according to the conditions in which that child is reared. Every child has the capacity to be taught. That is how it learns its mother tongue.

I have studied very closely how a baby learns to speak, and have tried to work out some method according to these basic rules. I call this "the educational method of the mother tongue" and I have used this method for teaching music.

Toshiyo Eto was the first pupil who was taught according to this method. Musical talent is something that comes after birth. In order to prove this, let me speak about my experience.

I let a newborn baby listen to classical music. For example, a Brandenburg concerto or a Tschaikowsky serenade or a Beethoven quartet. I choose one movement from such classics and let the baby listen to the same tune every day. In about five months time the baby will memorize this melody. If you do not believe this, please try it yourself.

It is very easy to test whether the infant has memorized the melody or not. To relate one of my experiences: A certain friend of ours had a baby. At that time its sister was six years old and she would practice the first movement of Vivaldi's G minor concerto every day. I visited their home when the baby was five months old. The baby was in a good mood and in its mother's arms. So I decided on the test. I played Bach's *Minuetto*. The baby looked happy. In between I switched to the first movement of Vivaldi, which the baby was always hearing. At the first three notes, the baby moved his whole body in time with the music and looked much happier. He clearly distinguished these two melodies.

We should try to let babies listen to good music and to nurture a good music sense as early as possible.

Let me here explain how a nightingale is trained to sing well. If we catch a very young, wild nightingale in the Spring and put a good-voiced nightingale beside it for about 30 days, the throat of the baby nightingale changes so that it will be able to sing like its teacher. By changing the surroundings, the wild bird will change in order to fit the new situation. If we use a gramaphone to train a nightingale, the bird will sing accordingly—even imitating the sound of the needle going over the surface of the record.

Almost the same may be said of human beings. Children listen to the pronouncing of words by their parents and their vocal chords adjust themselves physiologically to make the same kind of pronunciation as their parents. The pronunciation of English by a Japanese child and an American child is different. This is because the physical adjustment has not been made by the Japanese child.

To give a bad example: If a nightingale that sings poorly is kept close to a young nightingale for some time, the young bird will learn to sing poorly. This is one basic rule.

From my tests of twenty years, I have found that young children who have been given a chance to listen to good music acquire a good sense of music—just like naturally being accustomed to their mother tongue. We should realize that even a child of six has been receiving for six years. From a musical point of view, the child can be educated by good music, bad music, or no music at all.

When we teach the violin to a six-year-old child, we have to admit there is a difference in musical abilities. There are children who learn quickly and children who are rather slow. Most people seem to think that the difference is because of the musical talent (or inheritance) of the child, but I do not wholly agree with this. I think that we should remember that the child is getting education from the time it is born. In Talent Education, we warn all parents that education can not be started too soon. Our motto is: the sooner, the better.

Another basic rule is: If we do not educate at all, the child will learn nothing. For instance, the talent for music can only be had by cultivating it and can not be achieved by itself. This is my conviction.

If music talent could be acquired naturally, the cultural history of mankind would have been quite different, I am sure. Children born in the Stone Age were educated under a low degree of culture. Children educated by a high degree of culture grow up to have all sorts of talents. The level of the children of the Stone Age and of today is different. Children re-act according to education and it is up to us to find the best method of education.

The seed for music should be sown early by this new method, Talent Education, so that it will turn out to be a talent after the child has grown up.

Let us think of how talent is cultivated. I like to use the phrase "capacity of the brain" to mean the capacity to achieve talent and to use it. To discover the "capacity of the brain" is one point we have yet to solve in all the problems we have in regard to education. Scholars of heredity may say that the talents for music, mathematics or literature are there when the baby is born, but I wish to disagree on this point. My reason is that the matter of heredity is within the limit of psychological conditions, whereas culture, built up by mankind, cannot be passed on, physically.

I wish to define the meaning of the phrase "brain capacity" to mean the ability to catch one's surroundings and to realize it. In other words, to take in things outside of oneself and to work it into a sort of energy within one's self and bring it out by actions. In this sense, what I wish to call superior heredity will mean more speed and delicacy in catching things outside oneself. Brains that have no speed or are dull are what I consider inferior heredity. I wish to divide the classification of heredity by the above standard. That, I believe, is the reason why the result is not the same even when the children are educated under the same conditions.

This is to say that a child with good heredity will not

grow up to be a highly educated man if his education is only on the same level with that of the Stone Age. It is only with high educational levels that well-educated man can be made. History tells us that this is true and I believe the same may be said for the future. Because we do not know the future standard of civilization, we cannot estimate how high an education the new born child will be able to receive and achieve. The capacity and possibilities are so great. I like to call this "the unlimited height."

All parents interested in Talent Education should look upon their children with this thought always in mind. So, in educating their children, in whatever field it may be, the most important point is that the parents should realize that the child has unlimited possibilities according to the education that is given the child. This is what I wish to tell all parents: If your child has already started to speak, please believe in the bright brains and abilities of your child.

We must always be thinking of new and better methods in order to give a better and higher education to our children.

In cultivation, the most important thing is the seedling. The whole future of the plant depends mostly on the seedling—how big the tree will grow, how much fruit it will bear, etc.

Although this is a fact known by everyone, so few parents think in this way when the matter concerns their own children. It seems a pity that we do not realize and utilize this knowledge in regard to the education of our own children.

It is often said that children who are bad in arithmetic are stupid, dull. This is jumping to the wrong conclusion. Why do we not teach arithmetic by the same method that we teach our mother tongue? A child will learn four or five words and use them many times every day and therefore will be able to use them quite freely. Ability to use the words comes only from using them. A few words can be increased gradually and naturally. Then ten words will become the basis for the next increase. This is the method by which the mother tongue is learned by the child.

I have tried out my new method of teaching arithmetic at some primary schools. We taught about 40 pupils by what I call "The full-mark method." We teach until every pupil in the class gets full-marks (100%) and education begins from this stage. We teach how easy it is to get full-marks and the method we use is the same as teaching the mother tongue. According to our tests of teaching arithmetic for five years, we found that all pupils were able to get full marks, every time without exception.

This is the method I use to teach music. I think that success in education can be attained when all parents believe in the capacity of their children at a very early stage, and start education as soon as the baby is born. It will be a success when our society becomes this way.

The final objective of Talent Education is to cultivate artistic appreciation in a child, not to make a musician out of every child we teach. It is a movement started by myself and carried on by parents who want to bring up their children to have a refined human character. Please be eager and serious in the education of your child and give full cooperation to your child's teacher—this is my message to parents.

Any Child Can Be Tone Deaf

Any human being in the world will grow up to be tone-deaf if he is brought up from the day of his birth for twelve or thirteen years hearing every day only records of music played out of tune. This is for exactly the same reason that children in Osaka, who every day hear nothing but the Osaka dialect as they grow up, will all without exception speak the Osaka dialect as adults. For this same reason also, the children brought up in different regions all around the world all grow up to be expert connoisseurs of the delicate pronunciation and melodies of the speed native to the region of the country in which they were raised.

If a newly born baby is played a record of a Vivaldi violin concerto every day whenever it cries, the baby will have learned the concerto well after four or five months. The same thing is true if the baby is brought up listening to a Bach concerto.

This method of training is being put into practice today everywhere in Japan.

This fact entirely demolishes the common-sense notions that we have long held about the inborn talents of human beings, since it proves that there is no such thing as a person literally born with a special aptitude, such as an inborn talent for music.

This is because a person either becomes tone-deaf, or grows to have a superior appreciation of music, depending on the method in which he was trained, that is, depending on his environment. Therefore, we are left with the simple fact that abilities are gradually acquired through the operation of the adaptive powers which enable human beings to adjust to their environment.

The facts adduced above prove that this is not a question of musical talent alone, but rather that talents in general are acquired, not inborn.

Thus, the human mind, literary talent, mathematical talent, and other talents as well, are all developed according to post-natal conditions.

Life Activities Develop Abilities

Man is endowed with life amid natural surroundings, and lives his life adapting himself to his natural environment as well as to the cultural environment created by man himself. Thus, I believe that culture is merely a part of man's environment and nothing more.

Living beings must adapt themselves to their environments in order to live ; the efforts at adaptation are constantly accompanied by changes from moment to moment, and life is preserved while constant physiological adaptations are being performed. Therefore, in the long run, I believe that environmental changes also occasion hereditary changes by means of human physiological adaptations, thus actually creating the history of human life.

With regard to the idea that culture is merely a part of environment, I might add that a baby who is raised in an extremely low temperature and exposed to cold winds grows up to be an adult able to withstand the cold very well. I think that the same conditions apply to a person who is constantly exposed to the special air currents called music and who grows up to be a person with the ability to withstand music.

To sum up, we could express in simple terms what we have said above about the prime forces causing abilities to develop and the conditions for their development in the following manner :

1. What develops abilities ?   Life activities.

2. How ?   By adapting to the environment in order to live.
3. Why are there superior and inferior abilities ?   Because of inferior or superior life activities (through heredity).

Thus, in my opinion, the conditions mentioned above decide the way in which various superior or inferior abilities are developed in individuals out of their respective environments.

For this reason, if a person with highly superior life activities is born in the Stone Age and brought up in a Stone Age environment, he will, despite his superior potentialities, grow up into a person with abilities appropriate to the Stone Age. Even a person with far inferior life activities to the Stone Age man will grow up to be a person with incomparably higher cultural abilities if he is raised in the environment of the society of today. On the other hand, if a contemporary baby, born in our day, were to be raised in an environment of Stone Age people, he would be entirely unable to display the cultural traits of today, but would grow up instead to be a person with entirely Stone Age abilities and sensitivities.

All Children Are Wonderful

All children everywhere in the world are born with wonderful life activities.

These wonderful innate abilities develop according to the training given them. They grow rapidly day by day, hour by hour, in conformity with the environment.

One day, about 30 years ago, the following fact was brought (home) to my mind with a terrific impact :

"All children everywhere in Japan receive a superior education in learning to speak freely and fluently the extremely difficult Japanese language."

The discovery of this fact was a startling revelation to me. My researches began from that very day.

To me, the all-important proposition was this :

"All children possess the potentiality of being trained to superior abilities."

And it is a fact that Talent Education in language has been given to growing children in every corner of the globe for thousands of years. All children are educated superbly in this way.

This fact reveals the following truth :

"If only they are trained skillfully, in the same way as they are educated in their own native language, all children throughout the world can develop their native abilities."

Until that day, I had been asleep in the common-sense notions handed down to me. But on that day 30 years ago, I was not only startled, but I also awoke.

Do Not Spoil the Seedlings

Many parents who do not know how vast are the human being's potentialities and how to develop these potentialities properly are unconsciously neglecting to foster their children's growth at the proper time, and are thus ruining their children. All growth begins from the very day of birth.

If the seedling is spoiled, nothing can be done about the sad fate of that plant or being.

Abilities develop only for things which have been experienced. But we must not forget how a seedling grows, about its fate, and about how it can be spoiled.

When we view growth from the standpoint of education, while we sense the wonder and the promise of something growing, we are at the same time struck by the fearsome idea that the momentary changes undergone by a human being in his formative period are irrevocable.

We cannot help being deeply impressed by the profound importance of educational methods for children in their early period of growth and formation.

When the facts were published at Yale University in 1940 about Kamala, the little girl who was raised in the mountains of India by wolves until she was seven years old, they must have given much food for reflection to all parents of children. Kamala, who had been raised in conformity to the life environment of wolves, had grown up into a human being with a wolf's senses, a wolf's abilities. After her seventh year she was raised by Rev. Singh, but in a period of four whole years she was able to learn only six words.

After the past has once been formed, nothing can be done to change it.........

One wishes to ask those parents who are resigned to the fact that their children are "not intelligent," what kind of superior conditions they have provided for their children, or whether, after all, they have neglected them and refused them opportunities.

If a child's abilities have developed well enough for him to learn to speak Japanese, then how can he possibly be an inborn ignoramus ? Inferior abilities occur when children like Kamala pass their formative period in an environment in which their abilities, except for language abilities, atrophy because of lack of experience. Their sad fate has already begun at this early stage.

Conclusion

Let us begin to educate all children from the very day they are born. The fate of a child is in the hands of his parents. Every child has been born with high potentialities.

The greatest duty, and the greatest joy given to us adults is the privilege of developing these potentialities and of educating desirable human beings with beautiful, harmonious minds and high sensitivity.

There is always a bright tomorrow waiting in the future for humanity. Someday, without fail, the day will come when all children in the world will be educated and trained to be happy human beings. I have not the slightest doubt that someday human society will be organized so that each person will consider it his greatest joy in life to live for the happiness of others.

When I think of man's essential readiness to develop into any type of person in accordance with his environment, then I am strongly impressed with the great love and blessings showered by Nature upon mankind.

Shinichi Suzuki ; President

Saino Kyoiku Kenkyu-kai

(The Talent Education Research Society)

Asahi-machi 1463, Matsumoto-shi, Nagano-ken, Japan

TALENT EDUCATION

for the happiness
of all children

by
SHINICHI SUZUKI

Since 1946, nearly 15,000 Japanese children have studied violin under Talent Education. A National Concert has been held every year since 1955 with as many as 1500 of the youngsters in a major city in Japan. We hope that children from the U.S.A. and other countries will soon join with us to make this an International Concert!... M. Honda, M.D., Ph.D., Director, Talent Education.

I consider it a great honor to have been invited by many progressive American universities and other institutions to take part in demonstrating a method by which the tremendous potentiality inherent in all children can be developed.

If I had said twenty years ago that I was going to have a group of over one thousand children, between the ages of five and thirteen, play the Vivaldi Concerto or the Bach Double Concerto, I doubt that a single person would have believed me.

Right after the war, when there were still many remains of destroyed buildings all over the cities of Japan, I started this movement because I realized how much these innocent children were suffering from the dreadful mistake committed by the adults. These precious children had absolutely no part in the war and yet were the ones suffering most severely, not only in the lack of proper food, clothing and a home in which to live, but more important, in their education.

I was teaching music before the war and found to my amazement that small children develop their abilities far beyond what their parents or the world expect of them. As long as they have a normal mental ability to learn, it has been proven that any child can be taught to appreciate music.

However, the success of this application is based on the following points: 1) The earlier the better, not only for music, but for all learning. Young children have a natural ability to conform to their environment. Therefore, if we miss this period of life, it is more difficult to administer the program and obtain the same kind of results; 2) The individual is a product of his environment; 3) Repetition of experiences is important for learning. Watch a child learn his first word. His mother repeats the same word over and over to make him hear and ab-

sorb it. Soon these words will become a part of the child, and in a few years, he will speak his native language fluently; 4) The adult human environment (teachers and parents) must be at a high level and must continue to improve in order to provide a better instructive atmosphere for the child; 5) The system or method must involve illustrations for the child based on the teacher's understanding of when, what and how.

More than thirty years ago, I suddenly realized that all children throughout the world can speak their native languages with the utmost fluency. This linguistic ability is the result of a method which has been in continuous practice throughout human history. Why can't they learn music the same way? The method of instruction which I have been applying in my *musical* education thus far is nothing but this method of training in the native language. Therefore, I urge *the youngest students* (generally, 3 or 3½ years of age) to hear recordings of the music they are studying as well as the music they will study next. Perhaps this is in direct conflict with many teachers who oppose having students listen to recordings of anything they are working on.

However, my thirty-year experiment clearly proves that an ear for music is something which must be acquired by listening, and the sooner this is begun, the more effective it will be. Namely, an ear for music is a human aptitude which can only be developed by listening. Thus, I am certain that musicality is not a gift, it is an achievement. By applying this theory in teaching music, I taught Bach, Vivaldi, Handel and Mozart to many children. Soon the children learned to play many pieces by hearing the tune repeated many times and finally memorized the entire work.

The ten children here today are living testimonials of my thirty years' study. However, we are not teaching them to become professional musicians. I believe sensitivity and love for music or art are very important to *all* people whether they be politicians, scientists, businessmen or housewives. These are the things that enrich our lives. I urge you, therefore, to explore this new path for the education of youngsters so that all American children will be given the happiness they deserve.

An opportunity to explain Talent Education to those attending the Japanese tour group concerts was available in the programs provided for several years by Scherl & Roth, Inc., a string instrument company.

In his early workshops in the United States, Suzuki frequently drew a diagram as shown in the background at this session in Dallas, Texas. He defined **Talent** *as being synonymous with* **Ability. Preparation** *followed by* **Teaching** *will lead to* **Ability—Growth.** *The method of study is divided into three segments (circle): 1) Listening—Education for Musical Sensitivity, 2) Tonalization—Education for Tone, and 3) Playing—Education for Technique.*

10 Points for Talent Education

Teachers of the "Suzuki Method" must strive to acquire these 10 points.

(During lesson or hearing children perform, the teachers must be able to recognize at once which of the following points needs most attention.)

1. Listening to records is important to develop musical sensitivity. The teacher should urge parents and children to hear records at home. He must possess the potentiality to make them do it.
2. TONALIZATION.—The teacher must have the ability to show his students how to produce a beautiful tone with nice resonance of the strings (and to find the "sound point").
3. Teach a nice vibrato.
4. Arouse a feeling for good *musical* tempo.

5. Teach correct intonation. (1st Position).
6. Develop brilliant trilling ability.
7. Teach nice musical expression, temperament and feeling for tone.
8. Intonation: *All positions* exact and with good tone; be precise and in tune in all positions.
9. Teach good procedures for studying at home.
10. The teacher must be able to teach *every* child. Sometimes teachers say: "This child does not practice." It is up to the teacher to awaken the desire to study. That is a good teacher's responsibility.

Japan World Exposition
April, 1970, Osaka

Early Development from Birth

As one of the most important projects that mankind should undertake during this century, we wish here to make a proposal that every country in the world should set up a national project to guide all the young parents to develop their babies' intellectual and mental abilities from the time they are born.

We have demonstrated that human abilities are not congenital: it depends upon the way they are developed. Consequently if left unattended, babies naturally grow up to adults with very poor ability. This is the way of Nature.

The upbringing of the seedlings decides the destiny of the plants thereafter : ill-bred saplings are apt to have tendency of bearing irrevocably miserable fruits. We all know this very well.

And yet, people have been indifferent to this problem for mankind for a long time. They have repeated the same mistake of convincing themselves that their children are born inferior, even when their own faults or ignorance might have caused the child's inferior quality. This is not the suitable attitude we should take toward our babies.

Many babies are brought up by the young parents who have no experience in developing the infants' intellectual faculties and mentality at the most important time of their development.

Yet, Governments remain indifferent in this situation.

It is the most serious mistake in human history not to have taken any policy againts this and left the babies under ill-care at their most important time of "seedlings".

Let's train the child-rearing instructors

Any baby is an important member of the Nation. We should not remain indifferent to poorly educated babies because of the inexperience or ignorance of their parents.

We therefore wish that as an international project, Governments in every country will consider the problem of the "early development from birth". We suggest that Government should take up training and placing in every city and town instructors who will guide and help inexperienced parents educate their babies, and develop their intellectual and mental abilities.

If this be realized, the world will enter into the new and truly "good" era.

We earnestly wish that all the world will give serious consideration to this vital problem and will cooperate for the realization of the wonderful new world.

Every child has vast potentiality for education

Today at this United Nations Pavillion, about 800 children from five to ten years of age are going to play the Violin Concert by J.S. Bach and several others from their repertoire.

I trust their performance will undoubtedly impress you. They are not specially talented children but their abilities are developed after birth. These 800 Japanese children will show you the possibility that any baby's ability will be developed if correctly educated from birth.

Any child in the world can speak his mather's tongue. Why does he have such an ability ? We have studied the problem of children and their abilities for the past thirty years in the field of music, and have established the new method and philosophy that every child's ability can be developed. Today we are going to show you how high children's ability can be developed.

We sincerely hope that for the happiness of all the children in your country, you will cooperate to set up a national project for the "early development from birth" for the realization of the bright new era when any child's ability and mind will be ensured to be developed correctly.

Shinichi Suzuki
Chairman
Talent Education Institute

VITAL POINTS
for lesson and home work
of this year 1971

1

バイオリンを斜めに

バイオリンを斜めに　よい角度に
（一人一人よく調べて下さい）

The violin is held at a diagonal angle.
(Please study these photographs one by
one.)

——貴方はどちらですか？——
—*Which way do you hold*
your violin?—

バイオリンを水平にもったわるい姿勢
It is bad posture when the violin is level.

バイオリンを水平に持たないように

2

E 線を弾くよい姿勢（上の方）

E- string posture.   Good posture.

下の方のような姿勢にならぬように

E- string posture.   Bad posture.

3

よ い 姿 勢
鼻と絃と肱と左脚————直線に

Good posture
Nose, string, elbow and
left foot—all in a straight line.

————貴方の姿勢はどちらですか？————
—Which one is your posture?—

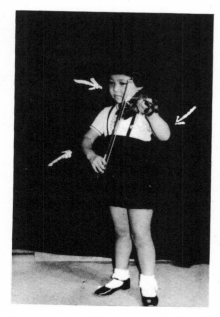

よくない姿勢
Bad posture

鼻は………！   *Nose!*

肱は………！   *Elbow!*

右手………！   *Right arm!*

4

移　　　絃
Change　　*Strings*

絃に弓をのせて　音なしで　E・A・D・G のアルペジオの体操

EXERCISE:
Rest your bow on the string.
Without making a sound, arpeggiate the E·A·D and G strings.

Study for changing strings:

Practice with both ∧ and ⊓ bows

移絃 の 練習

E——A

E——D

移 絃 の 練 習
Study for changing strings

弓を持つ親指と弓との角度に注意
― 親指の先　右の角で弓を持つこと ―

Be careful that your thumb forms this angle with the bow.
— Support the bow with top right corner of your thumb. —
NOTE: Always pay attention to the way you hold the bow.
This is very important.

＊弓の持ち方
最も大切です！

肱で移る移絃のよくない姿勢とよい姿勢との比較写真
—— 貴方はどちらですか？ ——

Study these photographs.

In one photo the movement of the elbow, when changing
strings is bad.   In the other, it is good.

—*Which position do you have?*—

よい 移絃

EからAへ移りました
○弓を移絃するのです。
肱を移絃ではないのです。

よくない 移絃

EからAへ移りました
○肱がこんなにあがってはよくないの
です。
上図のようにおけいこして下さい。

5

TONALIZATION

トナリゼーション

——毎レッスン指導——

正しい立派な音程を………音量を倍にして下さい

よくひびく

共鳴の一点の練習　完全なオクターブを知ること

注　意　ビブラートをしないで……

Playing with accurate and fine intonation....
Doublng the volumo of your tone....

GOOD RINGING TONE

A study for sounding the exact resonance point
Learn to play the perfect octave.

NOTE: play this without vibrato

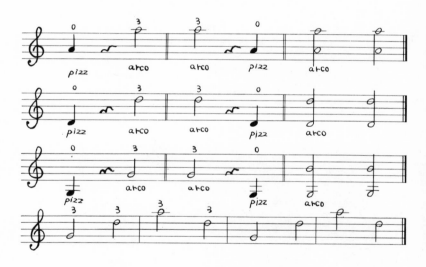

Train your ear to hear the perfect ringing tone.

6

This is an importaant ability
—Study the manipulation of the bow with the fingers.—
Using the middle finger as the axis,
please study the manipulation of the bow with
the thumb and fingers very diligently.
The tip of the bow shold not wobble.

Directions: 0, 1, 2, 3, 4, (see photo)
At 0, the bow is standing straight up.
With the top inside corner of the thumb,
increase the pressure on the bowstick.
Using the middle finger as the axis, relax the little
finger and move the bow to position's 1, 2, 3, and 4.
The entire bow should always be under control
when you play. The tip should not wobble.
NOTE: When you manipulate the bow like this,
the back of the hand should not turn to the left.
This is only an operation of the fingers.

これは重要な能力です

——指で弓を操作する練習——

中指を軸として親指その他の指で弓を
操作する練習をしっかりやって下さい
弓先がフラついては駄目。
操作……1，2，3，4（写真のように）
1は弓をまっすぐに持った位置です。
親指の先左角で棒に力を加え、中指中
心に（小指の力をぬいて）1，2，3，4
の位置へ弓を操作する。
いつも弓は先までピンと持ち、フラつ
かぬようにして弾く。
操作のとき手の甲が左へ動いてはいけ
ない。指だけでの操作です。

7

弓を持つ親指の能力をつくる毎日の練習（音は出さずに）

絃に弓をかるくのせて（写真のように）　右手中指と親指の操作を
中心に（小指の力をぬいて）
親指と中指の力で弓の棒を絃にくっつけ、1，2，3，4 とゆっくり
数えて、又ゆるめ、又棒を後にくっつける練習をくりかえす。
人さし指で押えつけてはいけない。
　　　――上級生は人さし指をはなして練習させる――
（注意）　右手の甲を左へねじらいなで、指だけの操作で。

A study to increase the power and facility of the thumb for
bigger tone. (Practice without any sound.)
Rest the bow on the string at the middle. (See photo).
Use only the middle finger and thumb (relax the little finger).
With thumb pressure, touch the bowstick to the string
and count "1, 2, 3, 4" slowly.   Repeat.
Only use the power of the thumb and middle finger.
Don't press with the index finger.
—Advanced students may practice this with
the index finger off the bowstick. —
NOTE: Don't twist the back of the right hand towards the left.
This is just an operation of the fingers.

8

上行弓 (V, Bow) の練習

肱と手が共に同じ速度ですすむ、V、Bow を練習すること

　○手先ばかり速く動いて肱の動かぬ、よくないクセの生徒をなくし
　ましょう。

Practice the correct movement of the elbow and hand on the bow.
They should both move at the same speed.
Let's not have any students who play this way.
NOTE: If the hand always moves ahead of the elbow,
it is not correct.

9

音量大きく、立派な音を鳴らす、弓の持ち方、鳴らし方

先ず、E絃で練習させる

—— 音量を大きくする弓の持ち方の指導 ——

前頁6の弓の持ち方、指の操作1，2，3，4の中の最強

4の持ち方で……弓先がしっかりと少しも動かぬ弓で

E絃を立派な音で鳴らす。

Producing a fine tone with big volume.
How to hold the bow.   How to produce good tone.
First of all, have the students study on the E string.

—Guide for producing a big   tone with the proper bow hold. —
Review the bow manipulations on page 6.
Using position ♯4, which is the strongest of all positions
1, 2, 3, and 4, produce a good tone on the E string.
Make sure that the tip of the bow is always firmly under
control, without any unnecessary movements.

上記の音量大きく美しい音の練習をしてから、アレグロのメロディーを
練習させる。

After producing a good tone with the exercise above, practice
the" Allegro" melody.

（指導）　1，2，3，4，の4の持ち方のままで弾くのです。途中持ち方
がゆるんでしまってはいけないのです。

(Guide)—   Of the positions 1, 2, 3, and 4, play this with position
♯4. Don't loose this bow hold while playing the study.

10

G絃を弾く姿勢と右手　美しく音量大きく鳴らす方法
——右手の移絃の形と弓の持ち方——
（注意）　弓を水平に通すこと…写真のように

The G-string playing posture and the right hand.
The method for producing a big and beautiful tone.
—The form of the right hand for changing strings and
the correct bow hold.—
NOTE:　The bow moves horizontally as in
the photograph.

The Law of Ability and the "Mother Tongue Method" of Education

It was forty years ago when this astonishing fact occurred to me. Children everywhere in the world were speaking in their own language; moreover, they did this fluently, which required a very high level of proficiency. "What was this all about?" I asked myself. People generally have believed that a child who makes poor grades in school was just born that way. "Brainless and dull witted" was the common and unthinking reproof. And yet these same children, unless born with brain damage, found no difficulty in speaking such a complicated language as Japanese fluently. If they really had been brainless they would not have had the ability to speak as they did. What did it signify? Why did it appear that the 'mother tongue' ability could be taught with the greatest of ease to every child (that is, the ability to speak, to make the necessary sounds in the correct context, and not the ability to handle the intricacies of grammar), and yet why did they not do well in various subjects at school, acquiring this learning just as they did their language? What is this ability? Can it be acquired, or is it inborn? To inquire further, what does inborn mean? Is it really true that talent for such things as music, literature, painting or any of the other arts is inborn? Like everyone else, I believed at that time, forty years ago, that if a child did badly at school, he was either lazy, dull–witted, or brainless. And I also believed that talent was inborn.

*   *   *

From that very day I started to study this problem and observe the practicability of the "Mother Tongue" method :

- *The environmental conditions and their influence on the new–born baby as it accustoms itself to the sounds of the 'mother tongue'.*
- *Teaching the child by constant repetition to utter its first sound. Usually 'mama mama mama' and so on.*
- *Everyday attitude of the parents after the baby starts to talk.*

— 3 —

‒ *Natural progress through daily practice.*

‒ *The skillfulness with which the parents build up enthusiasm in the child,
and the happiness the child finds in acquiring its newfound ability.*

*As a result I learned that the natural method of teaching a child its mother
tongue is a marvelous educational process. It fills the child with enthusiasm.
It is a natural process in which practice continues from morning till night.
The child feels none of the anguish that so often accompanies learning by
conventional methods which are applied to other forms of education. What
child would refuse to learn its "mother tongue", that is, quit this means of
communication, because they found the routine dull? Every child in such an
environment grows steadily and without mishap toward an involvement in
this delightful ability, and responds according to the stimuli supplied it by the
parents.*

*With this method, what human abilities might be developed! Superior en-
vironment; skill to build up enthusiasm; joy in practice and more practice.
Surely the "Mother Tongue" method is the most outstanding example of the
development of human ability.*

‒ ‒ *Experimental Class at Regular School* ‒ ‒

*Some time later I tried to adapt this method to music education for young
children. I accepted a number of children without first auditioning them, and
began to teach them violin experimentally, convinced that every child would
develop. The children did show great progress and enjoyed the process. What
has happened to those children of forty years ago, and how active they are now
in all parts of the world, will be reported in a later chapter. Anyhow, the
"Mother Tongue" method was capable of being adapted to music education as
well as other lines of learning, and I felt more and more confident that this*

concept would stand the test of time.

*   *

Twenty-five years ago, I very eagerly wanted to have a school experiment conducted, using my "Mother Tongue" method in their daily routine, and I asked Principal Kamijo of a primary school in Matsumoto if he might try it out. He graciously acceded to my request and the experiment in education was launched.

The school had four groups in first grade, and one was chosen as the experimental group. I suggested that no one should be 'failed', no drop-outs allowed, and one of the teachers, a Mr. Tanaka, was put in charge and the experiment was underway.

There was one child who could not even count up to three; she seemed to be somewhat retarded, but I did observe that she was speaking her native tongue with ease. I asked Mr. Tanaka not to fail her and I explained my method to him. He understood very well and saw this child through her difficulties so that by the time she reached fourth grade she was no different from any of the other children in a class of forty. Later she passed her entrance examination for high school, which presents no small challenge in Japan, where high school entrance examinations are highly competitive. This experiment, carried out in a regular primary school in Matsumoto, by regular teachers, certainly proved that it is possible to educate in primary school in such a way that no child need be dropped from a class.

It was clear that each child could develop his own abilities very successfully by the use of this method. In this class the following things were observed: No homework was assigned; the knowledge was absorbed to the degree that it became an unconscious effort, (each child 'made it his own' so to speak); the lessons were performed in an enjoyable atmosphere, and, most important of all, no child was ever made to feel inferior.

— 5 —

Unfortunately this class had to be abandoned after some four years, for Principal Kamijo died, and his successor had no belief in, or sympathy with the experiment, despite the urgent pleas of the parents and the children alike. The group was broken up and spread among the other classes, reverting to what was, in the eyes of the new principal, I have no doubt, a more conventional approach to education.

-- Talent Education at Yoji Gakuen --

Next I would like to report on the experimental pre-school (that is, pre-primary school) methods we conduct at Talent Education Institute for the purpose of applying educational methods that develop children's individual abilities so that the ability becomes an integral part of the child. Twenty-five years ago I founded in Matsumoto the Talent Education Institute for pre-school children, called in Japanese 'Yoji Gakuen', and invited Mrs. Yano, an educator in this part of the country, to start the project in this method of learning so that every child might develop his ability to the point where it becomes a part of him. The children were, and are, accepted without any tests. This school has been continuing for twenty-five years. There are sixty children in the class, comprising in age those of three, four and five years. We do not separate them according to age, which normally is done in regular schools, because we know very well that the three year olds grow up steadily under the stimulating environment afforded by the older children. In one year, they usually acquire the ability to memorize one hundred and seventy to one hundred and eighty haiku, and they are able to repeat any one of them clearly upon demand. A haiku is a short Japanese poem of five, seven and five syllables in three lines. Of course, we train them to develop many other abilities, such as physical education and the development of quick reflexes, writing numbers correctly, and reading kanji. Drawing and calligraphy are

-- 6 --

taught, as is English conversation. They are also taught to speak their mother tongue, Japanese, clearly and correctly. To do this we use the same training methods as are used to train T. V. announcers. To observe the enthusiasm and happiness of these tiny children is the deepest source of satisfaction for those who work with them. During the last seven years we have tested the I. Q. (Tanaka–Binet system) for the five year olds who graduate from pre-school to primary first grade. The average I. Q. has been near 160. In 1973 the average was 158.

The many parents who have heard about this school are flocking to enter their children until, at this moment, we are fully loaded for the next four years. The children who will be enrolled four years from now are as yet unborn.

To sum up: The "Mother Tongue" method leads the child, by repeated stimulation, to develop an ability and make it his own. If a young child is taken to Alaska where he is raised in the cold climate, the stimulation of the cold environment over a period of years will develop his ability to endure on his skin and over his whole body the frigid temperature. On the other hand, if the child's experience of the cold weather in Alaska is brief, then the child, on returning to Tokyo, will have only learned about a cold experience and will have not been able to make the ability to endure cold as a part of his own makeup. The child, educated to use this method of learning, will find that it can be brought into play in building other abilities as well. It is somewhat similar to the theory of principal and interest. Interest produces more money and more money produces more interest which, in turn, produces still more interest.

Now comes the physical side of it all. In the example of the child and his experience in Alaska, it is realized that this experience of building the ability to withstand the cold actually was a physiological one. I would like to think that the "Mother Tongue" method can also be regarded as physiological, the only difference in the experience being the difference between air and sound, on the one hand developing, through constant experience the ability to endure cold and, on the other, through constant experience of sound the ability to speak one's mother tongue. It seems to me that the interaction between parent and baby, the sharing of their lives, the parent's mind, senses, and the functions which the baby instinctively learns and makes its own, are also entirely physiological. I do not know whether this subject is in the field of physiology of the brain or not, but from my experience I am disposed to think so.

– – *Why So many Dropouts?* – –

The method and the aim of education must become different from that which the child regularly experiences in primary school today. And it cannot be repeated too often that the several abilities of the children must be developed to the degree that they form a part of their makeup. What is happening in primary schools is that set curriculum is adhered to at any cost without regard to the human equation.

Increasingly difficult material is forced on the children as a routine matter, and some children, unable to keep up the pace, become deeply discouraged, give the impression of being retarded, and eventually drop out. And too often, the parent, not being in the close relationship with the child which we stress at Talent Education Institute, is apt to dismiss this distressing situation, saying, "Well, he was born that way and I can't help it." Unfortunately this attitude is all too prevalent throughout the world, and it accounts, I am sure, for the number of underdeveloped children we encounter.

– 8 –

This underdevelopment is due to the failure of education at home, starting from the baby's first cry. If young plants are damaged, we know quite well what the result will be. If we damage young lives we should also know what the result will be. I look for the day when nations will give much more attention to this most important subject, so important to national well-being, and implement a national policy that ensures proper development. As I have pointed out in this section dealing with the serious matter of 'drop-outs', the differing abilities of first graders is a very serious matter.

Under our present system the children, varied in abilities, including the capacity for learning, are thrown together in one class and, as pointed out before, advanced without regard to their capacity for developing an ability and making it a part of themselves. This method produces many difficulties and frustrations for the teachers also. They sense that what is taking place is bound to produce a lack of enthusiasm in the child, a feeling of disappointment leading to complete indifference and, eventually, to dropping out. In our Talent Education Institute we teachers have a warning phrase, "To force the 'manuals' (the curriculum) is to produce the 'drop-out'." In Japanese the word for 'education' is kyoiku. Kyo means to teach, and iku means to bring up. There is considerable subtlety here when we become aware that "teaching" produces drop-outs and "bringing up" produces well balanced children, and that the two combine to make a child's ability his very own. We must realize that "Mother Tongue" method is what this is all about.

*   *   *

Let us return to Mr. Tanaka and his first grade at the primary school mentioned before in the experimental class, which was guaranteed not to produce or allow drop-outs. The initial lessons of the first graders were recognized as of vast importance. Just as in the beginning of learning the mother tongue, the start was kept very slow. Extremely easy material was chosen at the start, and all the children accomplished what was set with no mistakes and full marks. This was a start in building confidence and enthusiasm. He made sure that every child understood the material and made no mistakes.

He stressed, trained and practiced this theory of 'no mistakes'.

Further he realized, as we all know, that small children have a short attention span. Some children became bored or inattentive after five or six minutes. When this happened, say, in the math lesson he would immediately switch to language, and when the attention of a child appeared on the wane in this subject, still another was chosen. At the end or a year these young children had developed the ability to concentrate on any one subject for some forty-five minutes!

In language he would repeat the training five times a day for periods of five to ten minutes. He would first give them eight words to learn (with no mistakes), and when each child had learned them and made them his own, he would add two more. Thus they would practice the original eight along with two new ones. Additions were made in such fashion during the learning of their first book. When I was informed that this was accomplished, I went to the school to observe the class at work. The children sat with their books in front of them, but closed. Mr. Tanaka called on a child to read Lesson 12.

The child stood up and recited clearly and correctly without any mistakes and without recourse to the book. Then another one did the same with Lesson 17. During the time they had been engaged with learning their first book they had, of course, learned not only to read but to write. So he directed the whole class to write Lesson 18, which they did easily and well, and at a remarkably fast tempo. If this method, with which I had asked Mr. Tanaka to experiment, is used, every child will grow, full of enthusiasm, encouraged and fired with the joy of study, which will grow like a snowball of discovered abilities. I used exactly the same method in the teaching of music, producing no drop-outs. Every child can be developed.

-- *A Report on My Experiment* --

I started to study the "Mother Tongue" method and began applying it to teaching the violin some forty years ago, convinced that every child could be developed if taught this way.

I accepted children without first auditioning them and trained them along the lines of the "Mother Tongue" method or, as it is called in Western Countries, the "Suzuki Method". The first pupil I worked with was the four year old Toshiya Eto.

Next was the three year old Koji Toyoda followed by the Kobayashi brothers, Hidetaro Suzuki, Takaya Urakawa, and many others, all accompanied by their enthusiastic and co-operative parents. They all made rewarding progress. At eleven years of age Toshiya Eto won the prestigious Mainichi Shimbun award.

I have never pressed any of my young charges to enter the professional field. That is not my aim in education, but, at the same time, I have never deterred those who felt the urge, and many of the original students went abroad to study professionally with distinguished teachers in the United States, France, Belgium and Germany. They have gained high positions in the realm of string instruments. Toshiya Eto is known throughout the world as an outstanding soloist. Koji Toyoda is now concertmaster of the Berlin Radio Symphony orchestra.

Takeshi Kobayashi is concertmaster of the Czechoslovakian Symphony; Kenji Kobayashi concertmaster of the Oklahoma Symphony, Urakawa of the Bamberg Symphony. There was a time when the Japanese people were as-

sumed by Westerners to be most unmusical, and indeed, from the Western
point of view this was once true.

Never having been exposed to Western music they knew nothing of it.
However, no one had looked into the fact that the average Japanese child is
able to speak his mother tongue long before he can read it. As I have explained at length, this was the truth which gave me the clue to the so-called
"Mother Tongue" method of education, not just in music education, but in all
branches of training. My story of the preliminary experiment in the primary
school in Matsumoto makes this clear. Applying the "Mother Tongue" method
to musical education of the aforementioned group, among the first to be so
exposed, I found further evidence of the effectiveness of the method. Realizing
that every child born into this world has ability of one sort or another (that is,
of course, with the exception of those tragically retarded) and that the "Mother
Tongue" method can be used in their education, I have often pondered
whether or not if all nations and races were to concern themselves more with
this type of education, a much better atmosphere of understanding and peace
among men might be the end product.

We all know how strongly my very close friend, the late Pablo Casals,
believed in this ideal of brotherhood and the great part that music could play
in it.

– – *The Law of Ability* – –

In conducting observations, I have thought about what the source of ability might be, and have come to the conclusion that it is the great power of life itself. This great power of life governs physical growth. It imparts ability during the growth process, which responds to outside stimulation so that life can be sustained. This stimulation enables the child to develop his ability as a part of his make-up. This great power of life governs every function of the body, which is centered in the brain, an organ with capabilities far beyond any computer. I can no longer bring myself to believe in what is commonly referred to as an inborn talent, be it musical, literary or any other form. My forty years of experiments in child education have persuaded me against such a belief.

I have no doubt that people are born with hereditary physiological differ- ences, but I believe that a person's abilities grow and develop depending on stimulation from the outside. Babies, whether born in primitive times or in contemporary times, start at the same point and receive environmental stim- ulation according to their respective periods, growing up as adults suited to the era in which they live.

It would be true therefore, to say that a baby born in the twentieth century, but nurtured and raised by stone age people in a stone age environment, would develop abilities that would correspond with that age. I am often asked what I consider to be the limits of growth in a child's ability. I do not know what the limits are, but I am persuaded that the child's ability can grow to the level mankind can reach, by the time man's history terminates. As a practical answer, I would say that a child can, at the very least, develop all his various abilities to the high level of his ability in using his mother tongue. And this level is very high.

*   *   *

I have learned that musical ability is not inborn, and that it is possible to raise a child to be tone deaf or to raise the child to have superior musical ability. Imagine, if you will, a Mozart or a Beethoven brought up from birth to cacapony, to every variety of unmusical sound. My own observations tell me that we would not have had a Ninth or a Jupiter Symphony. Thus any child similarly exposed would grow up tone deaf. Children raised in Osaka, hearing their parents talking every day, grow up with all the delicate differences of the Osaka dialect, and those in Tokyo acquire a Tokyo dialect. There are only human beings in the human family, and the word 'genius' is a term of respect we apply to those who have made an outstanding success of the abilities they have acquired as they grew up under good fostering.

Some claim that, as a result of heredity, a person has it in him to be a musician, an artist, a writer; that the talent is inborn and, in some cases, amounts to a 'natural genius'. I just do not believe this. When one considers all the babies that are given the miracle of life and the power to live, it is saddening to see those who are improperly brought up, where their kind of education has failed them from the age of zero years old, without beneficial environmental stimulation, and who are judged by unthinking people to have been born that way.

It is an ancient Japanese custom to catch a wild baby nightingale in the mountains and place it in association with a domesticated bird, one with a particularly beautiful song. The wild creature from the mountains hears this excellent singing every day and in due time it, too, is giving forth the sounds it has been listening to. On the other hand, if the bird has for too long heard the croaking of the mother bird, then the capture of the little creature will prove to be too late, and the subsequent attempt to train it as described above will end in failure. This is another example of the Law of Ability.

In Japan there are thousands of babies who listen daily to a recording of the first movement of the Mozart Serenade for string orchestra. The parents report to me that it is not very long before a very strong and deeply pleasurable reaction is observed, and by the time the child is some four or five months old, it is responding to the music with joyous movement. In the same way, and at the same time, the baby is absorbing every emotion the parents display to it : 'The fate of children is in the parents hands. ' It is at once a wonderful and critical responsibility, since children absorb into their make-up everything from their environment.

*   *   *

Some children are brought up by parents who seem to believe that the proper way to raise them is by a regime of peristent scolding and bullying. In accordance with the Law of Ability, the children develop their own ability to be scolded and therefore, deveop resistance. It is a frightening thing, and the eventual outcome causes the parents to wonder why their child was born so obstinate. Of course the child was not born so. It has develped its own ability to be obstinate.

--An Appeal for a world Policy of Child Development --

In October of 1968 at the Assembly Hall of the United Nations in New York I appealed to those gathered there to consider the necessity of a world-wide policy of proper child develoment, education and care. I explained that every child is influenced from the moment of birth by its environment and that every child can be developed. But there is only one way.

In every country in the world today there are countless parents who, in

— 17 —

*ignorance of proper child training, are raising miserable, twisted personali-
ties. It is one of the most urgent problems of our time, and appears to be
mankind's major blind spot. When one considers the important part for good
or evil that this future citizen of the world will play, I am unable to understand why the nations forsake such a critical task.*

*I wish the countries of the entire world could establish and carry out na-
tional policies for child training and care as quickly as possible. When you
contemplate a carefully cultivated green field and think of the care taken in
the raising and cultivation of it, you cannot help but wonder that all that went
into that project should be denied to children ; whereas if they, too, received
the care that the field had received, they would grow up to be good human
beings with their respective abilities highly developed, who would build a good
society.*

*But the raising and educating of children must be founded on a proper
knowledge of how all this is to be accomplished. If the situation is left as it is
now, and we fail to raise the 'young plants' as they should be raised, then I do
not see how one can expect to have good nations in this world. Without good
people you cannot have good nations. As a national policy it is the first
imperative that instructors should be stationed throughout the country in the
cities, towns and villages, and that as soon as a new baby is registered at the
appropriate offices, the instructor should visit the family and teach the parents
the best way to bring up the child both in matters of health and in the
developing of its abilities from the very beginning. The parents should be
taught how to do all this on their own and have a deep personal involvement
with the child. The instructor would then visit his territory regularly, give
further guidance and assistance to the parents, and watch the child's development. If such a system were to be established, and if the children of the
world were accorded such care, guidance, parental relationship and sense of*

responsibility, then, I am convinced, the world would start to change very greatly. I ended by urging my listeners to give this very important matter their earnest consideration for the sake of children all over the world. I was accorded a warmhearted ovation, but I could not help wondering which country would be the first to take a step in this direction. I wish it were possible to believe it might happen at least by the twenty-first century!

Some four years ago I, along with Mr. Masaru Ibuka, Chairman of Sony Corporation and a strong believer, visited the then Prime Minister Sato at his official residence and discussed with him for about an hour the need for a national policy of child development. Although he displayed considerable interest, it is sad to relate that nothing came of it. If such a national policy could be carried out in as many countries as possible (and, of course, I would like to see Japan in the lead) I think that in twenty to thirty years a great change in the world would be seen. The love that parents have for their children would be awakened to proper child development through the guidance of trained instructors, and good character and ability would be promoted in every home. By these means I am certain that many children on this earth would be saved. When it is realized that babies can be raised in many different ways, it is clear that the manner of bringing up children is the responsibility of all adults in the world.

I would like to ask that scholars and educators clarify the concept that ability is not inborn, and dismiss the common error of assuming that failure in a child is due to its being born that way. Failure is not inborn and ability is not inborn. There is the story of the two little savage girls, three and four years of age who were raised in the wilds by wolves and, of course, behaved like wolves. There was nothing inborn there; they absorbed the outside stimulation, developed a wolf-like ability and made it their own!

One more request I would make is that educators study the "Mother Tongue" method and develop ways for the abilities of children to grow in the same manner as all children acquire the complex ability to speak their mother tongue, thereby ushering in as early as possible the age when the tragedy of the 'drop out' will have been abolished from our system of education.

I have already spent forty years exerting efforts in this direction, but as a layman, I can do very little. Scholars and professional educators with their great influence, can exercise great leadership in changing the world.

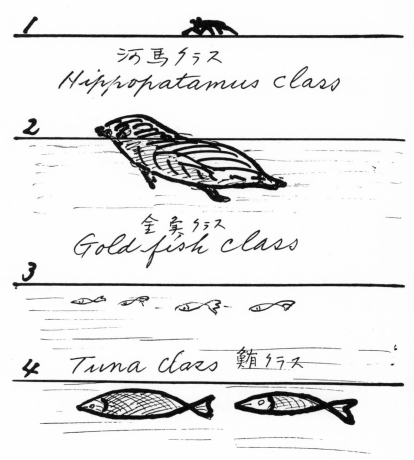

水すまぃ クラス
Water spider class

1

河馬 クラス
Hippopotamus class

2

金魚 クラス
Gold fish class

3

4 *Tuna class* 鮪 クラス

Suzuki describes tone in four classes: 1. Water spider class (a light, skimming surface quality); 2. Hippopotamus class (heavy, cumbersome, not beautiful); 3. Goldfish class (very pretty, but much too small); 4. Tuna class (most desirable, fine, strong, maneuverable, attractive).

Suzuki Method International Teachers' Convention, 1975

Topics of Study

Summary

Topics of Study Concerning The Fact That Every Child Can BE Educated

1. The Law of Ability and Conditions of Nurturing Children's Abilities :

2. Studying at Home :

    Musical ability of children will be excellently or badly brought about in proportion to their studying at home.

    It is very important that we should find a new way for their parents to nurture their high abilities with ease at home.

    As well as we should make an effort to make understand how to help the educational process at home.

3. Necessary Purposes For Music Education :

    (1) Nurturing a musical sensitivity :

    (2) How to teach tonalization :

    (3) Nurturing an enthusiasm to play and its importance :

    (4) Musical tempo :

    (5) How to make a joyful lesson in the class room :

    (6) Teaching method aiming at nurturing abilities :

    (7) Breath and spirit in playing :

    (8) It is our priority that we teachers should take good care of such children that remain in an under-developed stage, and open up a way to bring them up excellently.

Teaching Points for 1976

TEACHING POINTS

I. *Ability is developed at home.*

   1. *The Suzuki Method seeks a) to minimize trouble for parents b) to make lessons as easy as possible and c) to encourage the child's enthusiasm for practice.*

   Studying together should lead to the best and most effective ways to develop every child's ability. Let us all contribute our ideas and work together towards these goals.

   Please be sure to include the following points in the lessons you teach.

The Use of Cassette Tapes At Home

---

   1. *"Study with Me" cassette tapes.*

   2. *"Piano Accompaniment" cassette tapes.*

      "String Orchestra Accompaniment" tapes.

   3. *Record each lesson on tape and study with it at home each week.*

---

   2. *Parents develop their child's musical sensitivity.*

   Although the teacher may play musically for the child at his weekly lesson, the child hears this only one time each week. So this alone will not result in developing the child's musical sensitivity to a high level. The way to develop high musical sensitivity is to play recordings for the child every day at home.

   Teachers need to be sure that all parents understand this point.

   Bringing this point home is the responsibility of the teacher.

   It is helpful to make a tape of the same piece many times in succession.

   3. *Use of the tape recorder at home.*

   If a child can play well the piece which he was assigned, ask him, even if he is a beginner, to make a nice recording of his piece at home and to bring it to the lesson the next week for everyone to hear. A performance without accompaniment is O. K. Tell him also that at his next lesson you will ask him to play with the accompaniment tape. If he can play well

22

with it, he can go on to the next piece.

This procedure often works very well. It teaches the child a very musical tempo, and it increases the child's eagerness to play.

4 . *Teachers should have a class to show parents how to read music.*

II.   Classroom Techniques

1 . *Teachers must have their students play tonalization at every lesson.*

2 . *Let us all work hard on posture and on string crossing.*

3 . *Teachers should assign the next piece only when the student can play his earlier piece exactly with the accompaniment tape. (From Books 1—4)*

4 . *Young students should play with more advanced students to train freer and more musical motion and to build enthusiasm. Having the advanced students play second parts is a good idea, too.*

5 . *Find one important point to correct at each lesson ; concentrate on the one point which will improve the student's playing the most.*

Thoroughly explain the way the child should practice in order to master that point.

6 . *Point out to the parents the importance of listening to the recording at home and of practicing earlier pieces with the accompaniment tape. And, sometimes, have the student play an earlier piece with the accompaniment tape at his lesson.*

> *How to Determine a Child's Progress*
>
> A . *Beauty of tone ; perfection of intonation.*
>
> B . *Growth of musical sensitivity ; ability to be expressive.*
>
> C . *Correctness of posture and of string crossing.*
>
> D . *Desire to study.*
>
> E . *Ability to play in a musical tempo.*
>
> F . *Ability to suit his motion to the music in performance.*

23

III.   *Developing Enthusiasm and Ability*

1 . *About every two months, teachers should organize a concert at which all the children who have lessons on the same day are invited to perform. For example, children with lessons on Tuesdays should come for a "Tuesday Concert" at which they perform as a solo the piece which they can play with confidence.*
The piece should be decided about a month in advance so that the student and parent can work hard on it at home. (This is a basic point of the Suzuki Method.)

2 . *At least once a month, all students should meet for a group lesson. Students enjoy playing with more advanced students. They become eager to play, they play with more freedom, and they learn to play more musically from this experience.*
Choosing pieces which most children can play results in the most fun for all. (This, also, is a fundamental technique of the Suzuki Method.)

3 . *Students should be divided into groups according to Books for string orchestra practice. Cellists may be invited to join the practice sessions.*

IV.   *Tonalization*

1 . *The ear's ability to distinguish beautiful tone must be developed.*
Pluck the D string and listen to it resonate. Next, produce the same tone by drawing the bow. This builds one's skill to produce a resonant tone with the bow. (And listening to open strings develops the ear.)
The skill to make each open string-- D, G, A, and E-- resonate fully should be developed. Start with small bow strokes, and when a full, ringing tone is produced with small strokes, gradually increase the amount of bow.

24

2. *Holding the bow hair (close to the frog) and making the strings ring, arco, helps us understand how drawing the bow hair over the string makes tone.*
Listen to Casals' beautiful tone.   See page 13, picture A.

Next, hold the bow (but do not change the attitude of the hand or the height of the arm) and use the horsehair the same way to make the same beautiful tone.
Keeping the elbow at the same height, whether holding the horsehair or using the regular bow grip, is a very important point.   See page 13, picture B.

3. *Theory of Crossing Strings.   See page 14, picture B.*
How to study the principal idea of crossing strings :

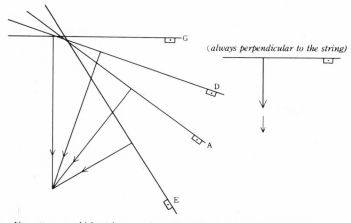

(always perpendicular to the string)

No matter on which string you play or in which part of the bow you play, this perpendicular force is the element which makes tone.

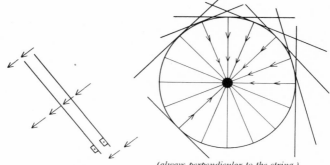

(always perpendicular to the string.)

Both the bow tip and frog should approach the string in the same way.

Control the tip of the bow so that it does not waver.

4 . *Tonalization*   *See pages 17 and 18, pictures G, H, I, J.*

   A. *Crossing strings at the frog. (This develops the fourth finger's flexibility.)*

   Note : Do not move the back of the hand. Only the fingers should move.

   B. *Crossing strings at the frog. (Relax the third and fourth fingers of the bow grip. Cross strings with the thumb, first and second fingers.)*

   Note : Do not move the back of the hand. Only the fingers should move.

5 . *Throughout the entire bow stroke the bow should remain at the same distance from the bridge.   See page 15, pictures C and D.*

   This develops the ability to draw a straight bow stroke. (This is good practice for the right arm.)

   To develop the correct right arm movement for a straight bow stroke please study the following points:

26

1) *The Kreisler Highway*

Watch the space (a) between the bridge and the horsehair. It should be the same from the frog all the way to the tip. (Be especially careful close to the tip.)

2) *Practice playing harmonics, using whole bow strokes. During this practice, too, the bow hair should always be the same distance from the bridge.*

Whole Bows :

G   string   D   string   A   string

6 . *Teaching the Down Bow.*

(Curing a Bad Habit.)

Some students begin the down bow by moving only their hands, or, in other words, they wait to move their elbows. Such students can only use part of the length of the bow ; and that is not good !

To cure this habit, ask the student to have his elbow <u>lead</u> the down bow stroke. This explanation will often improve the way he moves his right arm, like a Magic Formula !

Use these words to cure the bad habit which too many students have of beginning the down bow by moving only their hands.

The important principle for both down and up bows is that the hand and the elbow should begin each stroke together.

7 . *From the beginning of his violin studies each student should learn to extend his right arm over a point in front of his right foot.   See page 15, picture C.*

○   *Always ask the student to extend his right arm over a point in front of his right foot before he plays up bow strokes. At this time he should also learn to bring the tip of the bow towards the bridge by rotating the bow in his grip.*

This is an important habit to have from the beginning.

At first, the student should not draw the bow along the strings ; he should master the form at the tip and at the frog and the idea of movement between the two.

×   *There are too many students who do not extend their arms forward.   See page 15, picture D. Teach the proper form from the beginning.*

Students who do not extend their arms forward cannot draw straight bow strokes ; their bows travel in an arc. So that students do not develop this bad habit, teachers should make this point clear from the beginning.

8 .   *The importance of teaching vibrato.*

Often a student learns to find the resonance points on his instrument and to seek that beautiful tone quality. However if he does not learn good vibrato, his sound will only be half as good and half as musical as we would like.

Finding a good method for teaching vibrato is a very important goal for our study group. We must try to find a better way to teach vibrato.

9 .   *Please use the accompaniment tapes more. This year, throughout the country, all students should study thoroughly with the accompaniment tapes. This will give the children a chance to hear a fine musical tempo.*

To explain to students why they should listen to tapes, I often say, "Your brain is the con-ductor ; your hands are the orchestra."

Thought of in this way, the "conductor" is influenced by the excellence of the models which he has heard. We teachers should realize that we must give the "conductor" good musical ex-amples.

The accompaniment tapes which Talent Education has made available are very useful for practice at home to teach a musical tempo. In addition to tapes of the pieces, there are string orchestra and piano accompaniment tapes.

28

10. *Training Spirit and Breath*

"Tone has the Living Soul."

Training spirit and breath is the most important part of a music-teaching method. Bowing motion and bowing control are highly important abilities ; they convey spirit and breath, respectively, and thus they create many of our impressions of music. We can borrow the advice that Oriental teachers give to students of the martial arts of sword and karate. From early times, martial arts teachers have explained how to be relaxed and yet centered, ready for instantaneous action. They say, "Stand to your full height. Exhale a tiny bit and stop your breath." This will result in putting strength in the area of your center of gravity.

At lessons, if we ask students who focus strength in their shoulders or arms to put strength in the area of their center of gravity instead, we find that their shoulders and arms naturally relax. Please do not forget this teaching technique. It can be very useful.

A performance without spirit results in music without heart and tone without soul. Not only in music, but also in the formation of personality, it is necessary for all humanity to have spirit. Forming people who have spirit is one valuable goal of education.

11. *There are four points where we should relax the arm, four points at which we should not be stiff. We should teach students to be free and relaxed at these points : 1 . shoulder 2 . elbow 3 . wrist 4 . knuckles. (Take special care of points three and four. Too many students are stiff in the wrist or knuckles.)*

12. *We can often correct a student's form, especially right arm form, by watching him from behind. . . . So sometimes watch your students from behind. Be sure to notice the right arm.*

13. *Casals Tonalization*

We call the following exercises by the name "Casals Tonalization."

  1 . *Study how to produce a piano or pianissimo tone, as quiet a tone as you can make, with short bow strokes and then with whole bow strokes. Draw the bow steadily, with a "non-stop right arm," and produce a beautiful tone with this motion.*

  2 . *Then, practice how to give expressive nuance to your tone by moving your thumb and middle finger and by using an up and down motion of the right arm.*

  ○ *As you do this, be sure not to vary the speed of the bow.*

○ *The weight of the bow on the string is varied by the horsehair's elastic power and your desire for forte and for piano. (As pictured above.)*

○ *This is a basic teaching technique. Practice Casals Tonalization thoroughly, please.*

○ *The wrist and the elbow should move the bow together.*

14. *How to increase the ability to use the thumb and middle finger.*

   1 . *Hold the bow straight in front of you, tip pointing to the sky, with just the thumb and the middle finger. Rotate the bow to the left until it is parallel to the floor, or in playing position, and then straighten it up again.*

   Do not allow the bow tip to waver, and hold the bow firmly. Develop these skills as you enjoy repeating this game.

   2 . *Put the bow on the string. With the thumb and second finger increase and decrease the bow hair's elastic power, without making sound. As you practice this, be sure to hold the bow in the way described in point IV. ♯2.*

15. *How to explain Resonance Points.*

   Please teach perfect intonation of octaves, fifths, fourths, sixths, etc. All of these intervals have a characteristic resonance. Beautiful intervals are perfectly in tune and one can hear their resonance. Beauty ; rich quality ; mellow tone.

16. *The use of "Tuning Tone."*

   —A preparation for double stops.—

   Please use pages 4–7 of "Quint Etudes" by Shinichi Suzuki to show the student how to develop good double stops.

Suzuki Method Report —1977— "Tonalization"

NO. 1. Circle training.

How to teach the circle motion of the right arm.

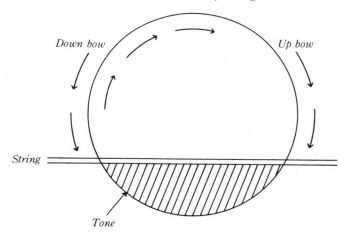

1. Without violin : Make a big circle with the whole arm. The tip of the bow and the elbow describe the same circle.
2. Next, make small circles at the point of the bow watching the tip.
3. With the bow-tip steady and the elbow making a circular motion it is possible to make full use of the elastic power of the bow.

* Please note :

The bow does not move on top of the string in a horizontal line. It must be drawn under the string by using the elbow's circle. This makes a warm, deep sound.

NO. 2. How to make the correct arm-posture.

Put the fingers under the bow-stick and hold the horse hair. Playing this way gives the feeling of the correct arm-posture to play the violin.

* *This is training to produce a big and beautiful tone.*

NO. 3. How to make the correct arm-posture.

Once this posture (No. 3.) is understood, hold the bow in the normal way using the same arm-posture. This will produce the same deep, beautiful tone.

NO. 4.   Staccato training using the elbow-circle.

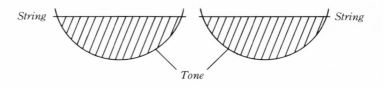

1.   *Without the violin : Make small bow circles.*

2.   *With the violin : Make the same small circles at the frog. Use the same elbow motion.*

3.   *When the elbow is high this makes small, hard sound. When the elbow is low this makes a big, warm sound. Practise both "p" and "f".*

4.   *Through these exercises you will improve the balance of the bow, the strength of finger-action and soften the knuckles.*

NO. 5. *The positioning of the right shoulder and arm to play the violin.*

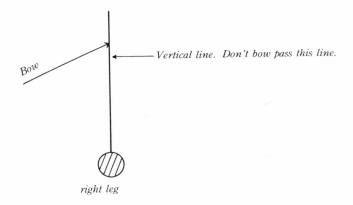

Vertical line. Don't bow pass this line.

Bow

right leg

Extend the right arm in front of the body. This is the correct position of the shoulder. Hang the arm naturally by your side. This is the incorrect position of the shoulder.

Hold your hands together in front of your body. Next, move the right arm in a vertical line. This line is the limit of every down bow.

This same position of the shoulder is the natural position for writing.

NO. 6.   Change of string.

Practise an arpeggio with no sound.

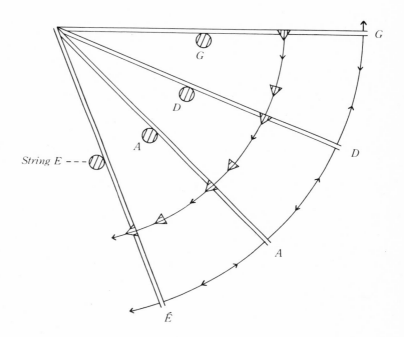

The bow makes the same angle with each string. This same condition on each string makes the best sound.

First learn to make a good sound on one string. Then transfer the same condition to the other strings to produce the same good sound.

The continued teaching of this technique and training of it are of the utmost importance.

NO. 7. How to teach correct change of string.
* Training of the finger-action.

A. *Do this exercise starting at the frog.*

   To change string, push with the little finger.

   Don't move the hand.

B. *In this exercise change string by using the 2nd finger and the thumb.*

* *N. B.*

   In both A. and B. use a quick and strong finger-action.

NO. 8.   How to teach correct change of string.
* Training of the wrist.

1.   *E-string to A-string.*

   With the elbow in E-string posture play the following exercise without moving the elbow using a wrist motion.

2.   *A-string to D-string.*

   With the elbow in A-string posture.

3.   *D-string to G-string.*

   With the elbow in D-string posture.

NO. 9.   Change of string using finger-action only.

1.   To improve the ability of the little finger and 2nd finger. (Practise using a ballpoint pen.)

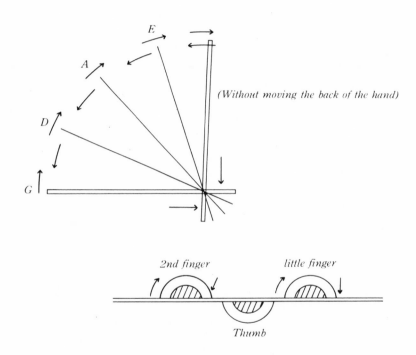

(Without moving the back of the hand)

2nd finger   little finger

Thumb

2.   Take off the first finger and do the above exercise.

3.   Put on the first finger but only rest it on the bow. Do the same exercise.

* N. B.

Put your relaxed right fist on a table. Lift your hand in the same posture and insert the bow. Don't alter the position of the knuckles to take the bow.

NO. 10.   An example of Tonalization.

Practise these exercises with a beautiful and big tone throughout the length of the bow. Wherever you are in the bow you should produce the same volume of sound. (Play on "Kreisler Highway.")

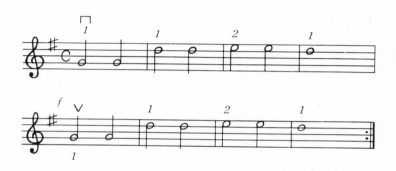

A.   Hold the bow at the tip and do this exercise.

B.   Hold the bow at the normal end and produce the same volume of sound.

C.   Take the 1st finger off and produce the same volume of sound.

D.   Take the 1st and 4th fingers off and produce the same volume of sound.

E.   Take the 2nd and 4th fingers off and produce the same volume of sound.

F.   Using only the 2nd finger and the thumb produce the same volume of sound.

G.   Using only the 1st finger and the thumb produce the same volume of sound.

* N. B.

Practise these exercises on each string.

NO. 11.   How to teach the finger-action of the right hand.

A.   *Training the thumb and 3rd finger.*

B.   *Training the 2nd and 3rd fingers and thumb to move the bow without moving the knuckles.*

NO. 12. How to produce the same volume on both down and up bows.

Down bow : Use 3rd finger and thumb.

Up   bow : Use 2nd finger and thumb.

Make the same volume on both down and up bows. Even though all fingers are on the bow you must only feel 3rd finger on the down-bow and 2nd finger on the up-bow.

Similarly, when you walk you have the same balance on each leg.

* *Note.*

R·······*Ring finger (3rd finger)*

M······*Middle finger (2nd finger)*

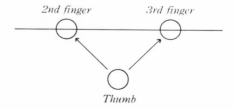

NO. 13. Casals' Tonalization.
—How to vary the volume of sound—

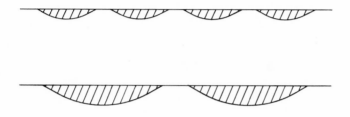

A.   Play "PP" for the whole length of the bow.

B.   Without changing the speed of the bow vary the volume of the tone.

*   To do these you must use central power (pressure of thumb and 2nd finger) in conjunction with elbow circle movement.

*   Casals' Tonalization······A temporary name for now.

*   N. B.

   This technique enables you to sing melodies with violin.

NO. 14. Staccato Tonalization.

* *Use the whole bow.*

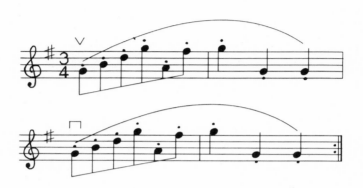

* *Down-bow staccato.*

   Teach the correct elbow posture. Most important is the vertical i. e. not horizontal motion of the elbow. This motion combined with pressure of 2nd finger and thumb creates the same staccato as in up-bow.

* *Up-bow staccato.*

   Elbow down. Use 2nd finger and thumb to make each staccato note. This training gives a beautiful staccato tone.

   Practise until you can produce the same tone in both up and down bows.

NO. 15.   *How to draw a whole bow straight and thus how to play harmonics with a rich tone.*

To play harmonics you must bow near the bridge and parallel to it.

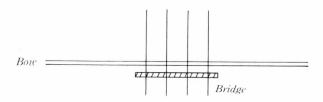

This diagram shows how near the bridge you must play with a parallel bow-stroke.

This exercise helps you to play harmonics with a full tone and teaches you to draw a straight bow. Use a whole bow and watch the bow carefully, so that it passes the same place near the bridge.

NO. 16.   *How to teach your pupil to play on "Kreisler Highway" for a big and beautiful tone.*

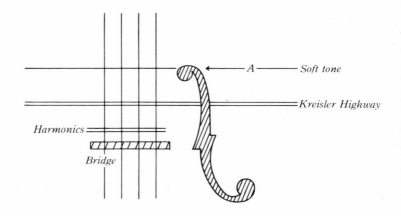

"Kreisler Highway" is half-way between the mark "A" and the bridge. To play on "Kreisler Highway" is the fundamental ability of making a big and beautiful tone.

To vary the tone-color by using a soft tone play over the end of the "f"-hole (Above the mark A.)

NO. 17.   The training of preparing the bow-angle.

Form the habit of preparing the bow before you play with the correct angle for whichever string you start on.

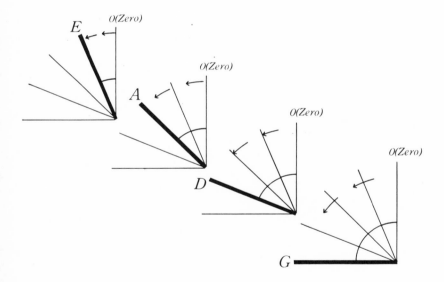

Use 2nd finger and thumb to manipulate the bow into the correct angle.
* *O(Zero)• • •When the bow is in this position there is no power and you don't play with the bow at this angle.*
This preparation of each of the four strings is very important.

NO. 18.   How to teach the correct posture of the left hand.

In No. 1 photograph the palm of the hand is vertical, touching the body of the violin.

In No. 2 photograph : Take the same hand to the first position. Don't alter the angle the angle of your wrist.

Practise this many times until the child really understands the correct posture.

* N. B.

The elbow carries the hand to first position.

NO. 19. Training of the finger-action of the right hand.

To teach the use of finger-action when playing fast notes.

* *Practise at the frog directly under the lapping.*
* *Only use the fingers i. e. not the wrist.*
* *These exercises help to loosen the knuckles.*
* *Practise until you can do this with no noise, only a beautiful sound.*

NO.20.   Training of correct arm motion, (elbow)

(Every body must do 10,000 times only!)

E string

D string

also G.string A string

* *The elbow moves up and down.*

Where the arrows are marked in this exercise take the bow off the string and move rapidly up and down several times using the elbow.

Afterwards play this scale. (G.and A major also)

Developing Children's Ability Using the Suzuki Method How We Are Doing Now 1977

"Every child can be developed in his ability.
Let's pursue the right teaching method."

by Shinichi Suzuki

The Suzuki Method is another name for the Mother Tongue Method. In this coming Second International Conference on the Suzuki Method, we intend to have an international cooperative study to discuss a better method of teaching music to children; a more natural method by which the ability of every child can be developed properly and successfully; a method based on the Mother Tongue teaching method by which all children of the world are developed to a great extent with a good awareness of the law of ability. "The dawn of the world begins with children."

There certainly exists a method by which every child can be developed in his ability. Because of the fact the children all over the world prove their ability in learning their own mother tongue, we firmly believe that ability is not inherited, but is possible to be equally acquired by every child. However, to our great sorrow, because of wrong teaching methods, human beings have failed in their attempts to fully develop children's high potentiality with the only exception being the mother tongue acquirement method. What's worse, people have failed to realize their own faults in that they have used the wrong methods for teaching children, and attributed their failure to the lack of inherent ability in the children. That is the history of ignorance and thoughtlessness of human beings in the past. They have made a serious mistake, but now is the time when we should go ahead and shift to a new era of awakening for humanity, holding this firm belief, and love for humanity, as the pioneers of a new era in which every child can be developed properly. Let us pursue and develop the method through which all children can be fully developed in their ability. I ask all of you, let us join together hand in hand and make an effort to improve our methods continuously. First pursuing a more effective teaching method of music, then extending to a wider educational revolution.

This Second International Conference is to be held with the sole object of strengthening this aim and deepening our mutual friendship. I hope this object will be attained successfully through the efforts of all participants.

In the Conference, we are expecting the presentations of reports of study and research on some new ideas by teachers from all parts of the world. For your information, let me introduce here, the latest report on the teaching methods in Japan since the last meeting.

1. Children's ability is developed at home :

During the lesson the teacher observes his or her students and finds out the most important and essential point for the child to learn. The teacher lets the child understand how to practice it, and gives the point as homework to complete by the following lesson. If the teacher gives two or three points as homework at one time, the results will be unsuccessful. "One point for one lesson" is the most effective method.

In the lesson room, three or four students may be waiting for their turn, watching their friends having their lessons. They will influence each other in this way and make better progress. A one-to-one lesson in the room is not as successful in stimulating the learning motivation. The lesson in the class room is the occasion for teachers to coach their students. Their ability will be developed successfully by their accumulated willingness to practice at home. Therefore, it is necessary for the teachers to make efforts to obtain full understanding from the children's mothers and at the same time to cultivate and develop a teaching method that minimizes the requirement for help from the mothers. For this purpose, the following ways and techniques have been tried with satisfying effects.

2. Utilization of cassette tapes :

I consider the invention of the cassette tape recorder as a revolutionary tool for music education, and Japanese members are making the most use of them. I have made such cassette tapes as the following :

1) *"Practice with me."*

With the tapes, children are supposed to enjoy practicing at home with me, one piece at a time. Then children can manage to play the whole piece after part-practicings that they have played over and over with my tapes. If they can finish the piece satisfactorily, they may proceed to the next stage where the piece is recorded with accompaniment on the piano. This tape has been widely welcomed. It has spared the mothers trouble while children have been enjoying more practice.

2) *Accompaniment tapes.*

I made another kind of tape with piano accompaniment for Suzuki School Vol. 1. To the accompaniment on the tapes, children practice the pieces, learning the musical best, and gradually mastering the correct musical tempo. When the teacher judges that a child has practiced one piece enough, through and through, he says to the child, "At the next lesson, please let me hear you play the piece with the accompaniment on the tape." The child can proceed to the next piece if he or she can play well enough with the accompaniment. Otherwise the student is not allowed to go on to the next piece. This method has brought out marvellous results.

3) *Recording the lesson.*

Our children are supposed to attend their lesson with their own tape recorders so that they can tape the lesson and take the tape home for their practice. Thus I can say that the utilization of cassette tapes in the way stated above has proved to be very effective.

3. Importance of Tonalization:

The research and teaching of Tonalization is the most important aspect of our method. As a matter of fact, the quality of teaching of Tonalization determines the quality of the students ability. For this reason we are doing our best in studying Tonalization, and seeking how to teach it effectively.

If a teacher of vocal music can not teach vocalization, he will never be able to teach vocal music itself. This is also true with Tonalization on strings. Therefore, together with our study of Tonalization, we put emphasis on teaching Tonalization in the lesson. In teaching not only string instruments, but also musical instruments in general, the study and development of the teaching method of Tonalization is naturally an important subject for us, just like vocalization is in vocal music.

Development of children's ability.

As a criteria or an important part of teaching technique for developing the student's ability, we have made it our motto (in our study and teaching) that the quality of teaching depends upon how we guide students to develop their ability by playing a piece they are already able to play, with the emphasis on a very good sensitivity for the music, excellent tone, and with a good posture. These are especially important factors at the early stage of learning.

Developing the ability with a piece they are able to play well is one of the most important points of the Suzuki Method.

Accordingly, at the beginning stage in every lesson, children have to play the previous piece a few times to the taped accompaniment, before proceeding to a new piece which will be the assignment for the next lesson. They are also

assigned, as their homework, to play the previous piece to the taped accompaniment every day. As their ability develops, they come to proceed to the next
piece in a shorter time. Teachers decide when their students may proceed to
the next piece, judging from the student's developed ability, and accumulated
practices at home. If we allow the students to proceed to other pieces without
this procedure, our teaching will fail. As the pieces become harder, some of
the students may drop out because of their underdeveloped ability. If so, it is
evidence of failure of the teaching method. Every child can be developed in
their ability. To what extent depends upon how well they are taught.

4. Lessons in group

Once a month at least, all the children in the class are called together. They
joyously play together as many pieces as they are able to play. This is the most
pleasant time for the children, and at the same time, the best chance to
stimulate their learning motivation, to learn effectively musical beat, right
posture, and manners. Playing to piano accompaniment, or practicing duets
is their great joy and also brings out an effective result in ability development.

5. Solo Concert day

The last week of every other month is the week for solo-concerts. There is
no ordinary class in this week. On Monday, all the students of Monday classes
and their parents get together in a classroom for the solo-concert. On Tuesday, all the students of Tuesday classes and their parents get together, and so
on. Thus on each day of the week we have a solo-concert in which every child
is supposed to play a solo. Each of them is assigned, as homework, a piece the
child is able to play, to practice it hard at home, so that he or she can play the
piece on the solo-concert day. This is a way to effectively stimulate the learning motivation of the children. They all practice at home willingly and with

great pleasure. The solo concert is one of the important factors in the Suzuki Teaching Method.

Presenting Graduation Tapes

When students of our system in Japan are due to submit their graduation tapes, they follow these five steps, one by one:

Graduation Pieces for Violin Course

Step 1. Gavotte (Gossec)   *Suzuki School Vol.1*

Step 2. Bourrée (Bach)   *Suzuki School Vol.3*

Step 3. Concerto in g-minor, 1st mvt. (Vivaldi)

Suzuki School Vol.5

Step 4. Concerto in a-minor, all mvts. (Bach)

Suzuki School Vol.7

Step 5. Concerto No. 4, all mvts. (Mozart)

Suzuki School Vol. 10

Graduation pieces for piano Course

Step 1. Minuet No. 2 (Bach)   *Suzuki School Vol. 2*

Step 2. Two Minuets and Gigue (Bach)   *Suzuki School Vol. 4*

Step 3. Sonata K 331 (Mozart)   *Suzuki School Vol. 7*

Step 4. Italian Concerto (Bach)

Step 5. Concerto "Coronation" (Mozart)

or

Sonata Appassionata (Beethoven)

This system of assigning the graduation pieces has proved to be very effective in motivating student's learning, and this year we numbered six thou-

sand graduates in Japan. This system aims at student's efforts to turn in the tapes, and the teacher's efforts to stimulate their students' learning motivation. Actually our teachers permit their own students to graduate, and the president authorizes it. Therefore, no students who submitted the tapes can fail to graduate. We make it a rule that graduation certificates are granted to all of the students who submit the tapes. Graduation ceremonies are held locally in each classroom all over the country, at which the certificates are given to the students by their own teachers, and then a graduation concert takes place. For the children, to have a goal that can be reached through their own efforts is a great joy and brings out very fruitful results. I hope that this graduation system will be introduced to countries all over the world. This system is also a very important aspect of the Suzuki Method.

Every year the level of children's development is elevated higher. This year we had two seven-year-old graduates in the violin course who performed the Mozart's concerto No. 4 excellently . They both began the violin at the age of three.

This year we had the 25th graduation ceremony, that is, we have been carrying on the system for twenty-five years.

6. Summer School

Every year in the city of Matsumoto we have a ten-day summer school from the end of July to the beginning of August (five days for the first half, and five days for the second). This summer we are going to have the 27th summer school. As well as teachers from all parts of the country, approximately three thousand students and their parents will attend the school. As a part of the annual events, the summer school is a welcomed feature for the students, where they can improve in their studies. The students who attended the school have shown improvement, not only in their studies but also in their person-

ality growth.

I am very much pleased by the fact that this summer school system has been conducted in the United States and Canada. In the States the summer school last year was conducted on a large scale in seventeen different places.

7. Teachers' Conference

Every May our teachers get together, give presentations of their new ideas, teaching techniques, and methods, study together and have practical training for the period of five days. This year we are planning to hold the Second International Conference on the Suzuki Method in Hawaii, and we will have many presentations of new teaching techniques and methods, cooperative studies, and practical training on an international scale.

I sincerely hope that we, together with the teachers from all parts of the world, will try to do our best in studying this method and having our daily teaching become as close as possible to the Mother Tongue Method, by which we can develop the ability of all children without failure.

A Petition for an International Policy for Nurturing Children from Zero Years of Age

by Shinichi Suzuki

Written for the
International Society for Music Education
and the
1978 Congress of the United States

Editor's note: *Essentially the same text was submitted to both bodies. Bracketted portions were inserted in the Congressional version.*

Members of the Society for Music Education, we appreciate this opportunity to speak to you about world peace and the welfare of all people.

I think it is a miserable and sad thing that various countries have armed forces and continue to increase the strength of their armaments. Somewhere on the earth there are countries constantly fighting each other and killing people. This is our history from ancient times. Many fine people have devoted great efforts to bring peace to the world. But in spite of that, the world is not changed. It remains in a miserable condition.

WHY?

The basic reason is that almost all of the children in the world are given no education at the crucial age of zero years old. We can shape the destiny of the children to become either people with beautiful hearts, or wild people like beasts. Very few people know this fact. Many people think that the heart and ability of a person is inherited. Presently there is no national system of education from zero years old, but we have an idea for such a system.

It is very clear that the reason for the miserable condition of the world is that almost all of the babies on earth are left without educational nurturing. They are left to drift. They fail in becoming educated as human beings because no country has a national system for education from zero years.

I know conclusively that heart and ability are not inherited. Ability is acquired by babies through the *Law of Ability,* and they adapt themselves to live and grow to the physical conditions through their great *"life power"* and its functions. I have proven this concept through more than 40 years of experience in the education of children from age zero.

Recently this same concept was discussed at an International Brain Physiological Conference. The idea was researched thoroughly and presented clearly. They stated that a baby is born in the state of a blank piece of paper, and adapts himself to the stimuli of the surroundings. The stimuli completes circuits in the brain and this makes ability.

The concensus of the world gives us the wrong belief that "our heart and ability are inherited." This wrong concept is still believed today, but it is the greatest mistake of humanity.

*   *   *   *   *

One day about 40 years ago, I was completely astonished when I noticed that every child in the world can speak its own mother tongue with utmost fluency. They show this wonderful ability of language at the age of 5 or 6. I then wondered "How does this happen?"

Please try to appreciate this astonishing fact. *Every* child can be developed very highly and successfully in their own mother tongue BECAUSE OF THE METHOD OF TEACHING.

I noticed that every child in the world has the potential to be developed very highly in faculties other than their mother tongue. It depends only on the method of education. The secret is in the "Mother Tongue Method." This is really a very clear thing that has been proven right in front of our faces. Yes, EVERY *child in the world can be educated successfully,* IF *we use the right method.*

Since the day I was astonished, I have studied the question "What conditions lie in the mother tongue education?" I had been seeking the law of growing ability, and I discovered the LAW OF ABILITY.

Every child's heart and other abilities can be shaped according to the method of rearing and nurturing. The method of nurturing from the age of zero decides whether the baby is superior or inferior, beautiful or ugly, virtuous or viceful I learned that children can be destined in *any* way.

As for music, I learned clearly that there is no inborn talent for music ability. If a baby were made to listen to out-of-tune music, then the baby would grow to be "tone deaf." The most important factor is the environment of the child from the age of zero.

Similarly, if you would put a newborn baby dog into a den of wolves in the forest to be raised with other wolves, then it would acquire a wolf's heart, sense, and habits. It would become almost identical to a wolf. On the other hand, if you put a newborn baby wolf in a person's home, then the baby wolf will become an animal like a dog. This is true also of human babies. A baby grows according to the *Law of Ability* and the conditions of the environmental surroundings.

I make this petition to you as educators. PLEASE MAKE THIS THE ERA WHEN THE INTERNATIONAL POLICY FOR NURTURING CHILDREN FROM ZERO YEARS OF AGE BEGINS.

If we leave the children of the world in their present condition they will have no chance to be developed. I wonder how many people there are in the world who have failed to become educated successfully. We must break out of the present day concensus of the world which believes that the state in which we find children is due to heredity and their inborn ability. In fact, these children fail because of our teaching methods. Please establish the system of education from zero years, and put it into practice—in order to protect, educate, and nurture every baby in the correct way. In this way no child will fail to become educated.

I have been teaching students for more than 40 years. In all that time I have never given any student an admittance test. I have been teaching them with the "Mother Tongue Method." (In other countries the name "Suzuki Method" has been adopted). Through my experience I have noticed that *every* child can be educated very highly. Since children of 5 or 6 can develop their ability in their mother tongue, they can develop their abilities in other fields as well. I have learned how wonderful children really are, and that there is a method by which every child can be educated.

*   *   *   *   *

Once, about 20 years ago, I shed tears in the middle of the night thinking of all the babies born on the earth who were in a miserable state because they were being educated in the wrong way. They were left without anything being done for them. I thought of all the human beings in the world as well. I got the idea that we should establish a national system for nurturing children beginning at zero years old from the tears I shed that night.

The system that I envisioned is like this:

A country should develop specialists for nurturing children. These leaders would go to all cities, towns, and villages in the country. When the government received a birth report, the specialist would go to the newborn baby's house. First he would congratulate the family, then he would give advice to the parents on how to educate the baby at home. He would give them knowledge on how to raise the baby, how to keep the baby in good health, how to develop his ability, and how to make this baby become a fine human being with a beautiful heart. All of these things could be taught through education at home, starting at zero years of age.

The specialist would have a geographical area of responsibility. Within this area he would visit every child until the age of 5 or 6. He would see how the child was being raised and help the baby by the authority of the government. Then, no one in the country would be improperly raised.

If a certain family was too poor to take proper care of the baby, or spend money on the health of the baby, then the government (either federal, state or local) should give financial help to the family.

We should have this kind of system so that every child would grow into a fine and virtuous person from being watched with a warm heart and educated in the right way.

*   *   *   *   *

We know that a baby has a wonderful faculty through which he can acquire all sorts of abilities. If a wolf raises a baby, the baby will acquire the wolf's heart, sense, and other characteristics. Every baby has this wonderful ability to absorb everything in its environment. I would like to stress that there is no fault with the baby. It is a matter of who raises the baby that makes the difference as to how the baby is educated.

As adults, we have to take the responsibility for educating the children, and we must solve all the problems in the present educational methods so that all babies might be nurtured correctly.

A new, revolutionized educational system is needed now all over the world. This new system is needed not only in infant education, but in elementary schools as well.

With about 40 students in the 1st grade, we clearly proved through our experiments in an elementary school in Matsumoto that *every child can be successfully developed*. We must only use the correct method, the so-called "Mother Tongue Method."

We must examine our methods of teaching, and change our attitudes in educating children. Then, we could not say:
"This student did not inherit any ability."
    or
"These students in elementary school are 'retarded.' "
    or
"Some students are not gifted."
Since even the "retarded" students can speak their mother tongue with fluency, they are already showing an excellent ability in language. The real problem is *how to educate the children,* not the children themselves.

Every teacher should study the *Law of Ability* and research this method (the "Mother Tongue Method") eagerly. In this way I believe we could educate all children successfully.

For over 40 years I have devoted myself to this idea, always hoping that the era of the new educational method would come soon. Please consider this problem. I think it is the most crucial assignment in the world.

Some children are still in an undeveloped state because their ability was not educated at the crucial stage, starting at zero. They have been failed *by* their education. On the other hand, some students have been educated very successfully. Therefore, there is a great difference between students. Some students are inferior and some are very superior. But the teachers in elementary school must take these children and educate them in the same room, using the same materials. I am afraid that the teachers have great difficulty in teaching them. But I believe that if a national policy for nurturing children from zero years old was put into practice, elementary school education would change greatly, and a new world through education would begin.

When the era begins which lets all children in the world be educated into people with beautiful hearts and desirable abilities, then surely armed forces and armaments would disappear from the world. Prisons and jails would change into schools where people would be re-educated into finer people. I am afraid that world peace will never come until we change the education of human beings.

The "Research Institute" in Matsumoto was finally completed this spring. In this building we will intensify our research and experiments on this new method of education. We will begin to educate specialists for nur-turing children. At this Institute mothers will learn how to nurture the children at home at the age of zero. They will learn how to nurture the children at home with no difficulties. In this way the era of a policy for nurturing children, which I have been working toward for a long time, will begin.

[Mr. David Smith of Atlanta, understands my ideas for this plan, and has helped me to finally realize this dream for the "Research Institute." I appreciate his kind-ness from the bottom of my heart. We will now begin to use this building to study the ideas that I have been exper-imenting with for more than 40 years.

Also through the kindness of Mr. Smith, we are able to present the "International Friendship Concerts." The concerts will be given in Washington on April 9th, in Atlanta on April 13th, and at Carnegie Hall in New York on April 16th. The 200 participants in the concerts consist of 100 children from America and 100 children from Japan. All of the children were educated through the "Mother Tongue Method." We hope that the concerts will spread international good will between the United States and Japan. We are very happy to be in America for such a wonderful occasion.

Half of the 200 students are children that can play the A Minor Concerto of J. S. Bach, and more advanced pieces. The Bach Concerto is a piece which students of music conservatories study. If we use the correct method of education, then we can develop even our very young

children to such a high musical level. It is our hope that
these concerts will let the people of the world know this
fact.]

Our purpose of musical education is not to produce
professional musicians, but to make fine people who have
high hearts, wonderful sensitivity, and fine ability. We do
this *through* music from a very young age. This is the
basis for our movement.

The children who are being educated with this
method do excellent school work and get good marks in
school. We have seen this fact through our experiences
for more than 40 years. We have accepted all children
without testing, and started their education at 2 or 3
years of age.

[I would like to express my heartfelt gratefulness on
this opportunity for the invitation to the United States,
to present these "International Goodwill Concerts," performed by 200 children from Japan and America. I want
to thank especially President Carter, and the Members
of Congress, and I plead that you would consider the idea
of a national policy for nurturing children from zero years
old. That is the reason for this letter. I believe you have
the authority to realize this important ideal.]

You, as teachers, must help the children of your
country to reach their potential through proper education.
I ask you, from the bottom of my heart, so that all children
of the world can be happier and lead better lives. I hope
that you will make every effort to make this—THE NEW
ERA FOR CHILDREN.

Thank you.

Shinichi Suzuki
Matsumoto
March 1978

National Suzuki Teachers' Workshop 1980

This Year We Must Develop All Students!!
Some Vital Points of Teaching For This Year

1. *Please be sure to make all your students use the study tape correctly from this year on for developing the correct musical tempo, musical expression and musical sensitivity at home. This is a new teaching method.*

* *The student practices at home with the tape and if the student can play perfectly with the tape in the lesson, then he or she can go on to the next piece. Please be sure to carry out this teaching method.*

2. *The teacher should put emphasis on teaching Tonalization in the lesson. It is obvious that the quality of the students' tone determines the quality of the teachers' teaching ability.*

3. *The skillfulness of the teacher in making every student practice well at home is the most important point of teaching. It is a reflection on the superiority or inferiority of the teacher. In the Suzuki teaching method, it is teachers' duty to pay attention to the student who does not practice, therefore, it is necessary for the teachers to make efforts to motivate students to practice well since their ability is developed at home. Making the children's mothers understand this fully and teaching them gradually to practice more and more daily is important. If you succeed in making every student practice at least two hours, then the ability will be developed. These are our responsibilities. Sometimes the teacher has to check the students' practice time at home and get the cooporation of the mothers, making every student practice for two hours every day. Tell the mothers that this is the rule of the Suzuki Method from this year on. Every child's ability can be developed. If you succeed in making the students practice well, then every child will be able to develop well. If love is deep, much can be accomplished. Therefore, be careful.*

4. *From the beginning of the lesson, the teacher must always check to see if the student holds the bow correctly. It is very important for the student to master the bow hold correctly from the beginning. I found many students holding the bow incorrectly. Please study how you can teach your student for developing the ability of the fingers to hold the bow. This is the teaching of Tonalization.*

5. *Please carry out the teaching method of changing strings correctly and perfectly from the beginning. This is the most important point. Please teach correctly in the lesson the development of the ability of the fingers to change strings at the frog of the bow. This is often foregotten, but this is a very important subject.*

6. *Although you are saying in a loud voice that every child's ability can be developed, your students have been developing poorly and they are not at the same level. Please be sure to bring every child's ability up this year. Therefore, very careful efforts are necessary. (This year there was a student who took five years to graduate from the 2 nd level.) Under this belief and committment, the Suzuki teachers should have the mission of proving the fact that every child can be developed. This is the subject of this year. This touches on a sore point, but it is not good just to say that every child's ability can be developed without actually putting the philosophy into practice.*

7. *Please study good teaching of vibrato this year. While listening to many graduation tapes, I was very surprised to find that there were so many students at the 3 rd level without vibrato. Let's make this our goal this year : To develop students all over the country who can play with good vibrato.*

8. *The study of tone—the study of Tonalization for developing a wonderful tone is the first mission for teachers. Daily study for producing better tone is most important for students' development. Tonalization is the endless world of tone. Let's go ahead step by step every day.*

DISCOVERY OF THE LAW OF ABILITY AND THE PRINCIPLE OF ABILITY DEVELOPMENT
—— *Proof that talent is not inborn* ——

by

Shinichi Suzuki

For many years, many people have cherished the common belief that talent is inborn and each person has his own inherited quality or nature, that everyone has his individual character and talent which are superior or inferior from his birth, and that this inherited talent cannot be developed further afterwards, if it is inferior from the start.

This belief has been advocated as a theory by many scholars, but I realized about forty years ago that it is totally wrong. Since then I have endeavored to prove that talent is no accident of birth and every child can be highly educated if he is given the proper training. I have demonstrated good examples of highly developed children in music. I also have been appealing for people in the world to understand my idea. It is very difficult, however, to change what has been believed for such a long time, but I have never been defeated by the difficulty, never given up my belief. I have proven the fact that talent is not inborn and I nurtured and developed many children whom I accepted as my students without any test for musical ability. I taught them to become splendid musicians. Meanwhile I finally found the law of ability after long research of the principle for developing talent.

I realized the following:

1. *Talent is acquired through the powerful function of "life force" (or the life-giving force or energy)*
2. *Talent is developed as the matter of physiology or brain–physiology which functions in a living organism in order to sustain its life and keep it growing.*

The law of ability might be summarized as the following :

"A living organism acquires talent responding to the environmental stimulation from the outside and adapting itself to all things surrounding it. Talent is the production of the life force ; therefore, there is no talent without stimulation which comes from the outside."

A newborn baby's life force absorbs all the things around him, such as his mother's way of speech, her way of feeling and thinking and so forth. We should notice that a child acquires his talent parallel with his growth through his life force, being fed with nourishment. A living organism would have to die if it could not adapt itself to the environment. When we know that talent is the fruit of the life force activity, we can learn that a child gains his talent in order to survive in the environment, adapting himself to all kinds of environmental stimulation which comes from the outside.

Through my experiences I firmly believe that the law of ability is quite true. It is an obvious fact that a child's ability is developed in a physiological or brain-physiological way, just as a baby's body grows physiologically through the activities of his powerful life.

If you move to Alaska with your newborn baby and raise him in the cold Alaskan environment, he will adapt himself to the stimulation there and will gradually come to the ability to endure the severe cold,. A physiological change will emerge on his skin over his whole body in order to survive in Alaska. Of course, one or two weeks stay in Alaska is not long enough to cause this change in the baby's body. He will never be able to gain the ability to bear the coldness in such a short period, though he might gain some knowledge about the Alaskan coldness.

A baby who hears his mother talking every day absorbs everything into his make-up and imitates his mother's voice, pronunciation, in-

tonation and accent, adapting his vocal cords and muscles around the mouth and so forth to the outside stimulation. Finally he becomes able to speak quite the same way as his mother, just like a copy of the mother. It is impossible for me to pronounce English sounds beautifully, because I was raised hearing my mother tongue of Japanese, not English.

I often say, "A person is the product of his environment."

Even primitive men who lived in the Stone Age had the potential to develop to a high level, but their potential was not stimulated by the environment more than the Stone Age. Everyone in those days, therefore, had to grow as primitive men of the Stone Age. They could not develop their abilities more than those in the Stone Age. This example explains the law of ability eloquently.

If you put today's baby into the Stone Age and raised it there, it would become like other Stone Age men. On the other hand, if you put today's baby into the future world of five thousand years later and if he were educated by highly civilized people, he would certainly develop to the same highly advanced level at that area.

I discovered the fact that the activities of the great life force can be used to develop children's abilities to a miraculously high level under good fostering from the very day of their birth. I would like, therefore, to emphasize the importance of education from zero years old. We should esteem and value LIFE more, and we should notice that every child has the wonderful potential to be highly educated.

Early Education For Young Children

Now I have to talk about education for young children more concretely. First of all, I can tell you how to surely make any child completely tone deaf.

A child who is raised by a tone–deaf mother or grandmother and grows hearing their out–of–tune lullabies every day will surely become tone deaf. The child's active life force accurately acquires the out–of tuneness from of his mother's out–of–tune songs,   just as he gains the wonderful ability of speaking his mother tongue fluently. He can absorb even the delicate accent of the dialect in the area he lives in.

Consequently, you can nurture a normal baby to become a completely tone-deaf child through making him hear records with out–of tune music every day——though I have no desire to try this experiment, of course.

I have the firm belief that there is no inherited talent for music ; therefore, we could make a child become either an excellent musician or a tone–deaf person according to the law of ability and principle of the life force activity. It was some forty years ago when I realized the law and I accepted two young children as my first violin students for experiment. They were nurtured by listening to Kreisler and Thibaud on records at home every day. One boy, who was four years old at that time, is now a professor at Curtis Music School in the United States ; his name is Toshiya Eto. The other boy, Koji Toyota, who was three years old, is now concertmaster of the Berlin Radio Symphonic Orchestra. It might be said that Kreisler and Thibaud were really their teachers, and I myself was just an assistant of the two celebrated musicians. The two boys were the successful products of my experiment on the law of ability. I would like to emphasize again that the great power of life activity is the mighty gift given to human beings.

A child who has no opportunity to listen to any good music gains nothing. If he listens to out–of–tune music, he will grow to have out–of tune abilities in music. If he is raised in an atmosphere with beautiful music, he will become a person of noble character, fine sensibility and

*excellent ability. I have been convinced of this through my experiences
of some forty years.*

*Now I would like the teachers who are using the Suzuki Method to be
aware of the following two points :*

(1) *What makes children acquire their wonderful abilities ?*
(2) *How can teachers and parents nurture their children to become
fine persons with high abilities ?*

*I have already tried to give an answer to the first question. So some
answers to the second question will be given in the following para-
graphs.*

The Law of Ability

*My research on the law of ability and the Suzuki Method was moti-
vated by a fact that astonished me greatly one day some forty years ago.
Children everywhere in the world were speaking in their own language with ease. They had gained such excellent abilities as to speak
with utmost fluency. "What was this all about ?" This must be the
result, I thought, that their abilities had been developed from the day of
their birth. Every child has a wonderful potential to be educated very
highly. I wondered why their abilities were so splendidly developed
only in their mother tongue. On the day when I noticed this fact I
started researching what kinds of conditions lie in the education in
which those wonderful abilities of the mother tongue can be cultivated
from the day of their birth. The method called "The Suzuki Method" is
the fruit of my research and the discovery of the law of ability is also a
harvest.*

*The following two points are the basis for acquirement through the
Mother Tongue ability.*

(1)*Some abilities are developed through hearing.*
(2)*Some abilities are developed through speaking.*

The same is seen in music education :
(1)*Some abilities are developed by hearing good music.*
(2)*Some abilities are developed by playing music.*

Abilities in music, therefore, will be developed splendidly if children listen to music and practice playing every day as enthusiastically as they practice their own language. Students who are hardly developed in music are the result of neglecting to listen to music.

If you gave lessons on speaking the mother tongue to your child and neglected to give him any lessons on listening, what would be the result? Up to now these same methods in teaching music have been used in general. Highly developed sensitivity in music can never be gained through this sort of method.

Every spring I have to listen to a great number of tapes sent from various levels of graduating students all over Japan. This year there are 7900 graduating students. Among them there are some excellent students who are five or six years old and yet can beautifully play all the movements of Bach's first concerto.

Th's year I listened to Bach's entire concerto recorded on tape ·by a four year–old girl who played with a little violin (size 1/16 th) very well. From birth she was raised to hear the violin played by her sister and brother.

Thus her desire to play the violin had been fully brewing before she picked up her tiny violin to start her learning. Then she showed wonderfully rapid progress and enthusiasm in learning violin, enjoying daily practice with her brother and sister, and growing to become able to play Bach's Concerto at such a young age. She won such a high ability in music through the same way as she acquired her speaking ability of her mother tongue with ease.

This is one of many good examples of children nurtured under almost the same conditions and processes as children follow unconsciously when they learn their mother tongue.

I have often asked mothers to make their children listen to records over and over again as their home work, but it seems fairly hard to put it into practice. Only a few mothers have accepted this advice. Recently, however, the number of parents who are able to understand the importance of my suggestions is increasing. As a result, some children are proving wonderfully that my suggestion is really right---through their rapid progress in learning.

The Building Block System

Now I would like to talk about how we can develop children's ability of performance. When we observe the process of language acquirement in the mother tongue very carefully, it is obvious that the ability of acquiring the mother tongue grows and is expanded effectively through the building block system.

A child learns his first word one day, and he repeats it over and over again until it becomes a part of him as an ability. Then he learns another word. After he has mastered these two words, he adds a new word to the two he has learned perfectly. He practices these words many times every day, then he accepts the challenge of another new word to master and so forth. This is the way a child acquires his speaking ability. The way of developing abilities in general is quite the same as that of learning one's mother tongue.

One ability is created first, then a new ability is built on it, and then another new one is put on top of the other, and so on one after another.

One ability which is sufficiently developed breeds another greater ability, and so on, one ability after another. Thus abilities are geatly expanded and become more powerful and functional. Teachers and parents should be aware of this.

This building block system is used by all Suzuki teachers, and children's abilities are cultivated and expanded steadily through this method. Children who are trained in this way, therefore, can play any of the pieces they have already learned, without rehearsal, anytime, anywhere. The children's memories also, are wondrously expanded.

Suzuki students must learn to play music by heart, and it becomes a habit with them. The teachers, however, teach how to read music also when their students reach the appropriate level. Until then they make it a rule to play without music in class. This procedure produces wonderful memory ability. A student who is trained by this method from the first and is developed in his memory ability can learn a new piece very quickly. Moreover, when he is taught how to read music afterwards, he can learn the music by heart in a very short time, and he can play it excellently without looking at printed music.

Through my long experiences I have seen many examples of children at thirteen or fourteen years of age who have acquired such high abilities of performance and splendid music sensitivity that they can play the first movement of Sibelius' concerto by heart beautifully and without any mistakes, after only one week of practice at home with the printed music. I have learned, through these examples, how wonderful it is to make a habit of practice without reading music at the early stage.

The Accompaniment Tapes

For learning musical beat and the correct musical tempo I made tapes with piano accompaniment for all the pieces of Suzuki School Vol. l. When the teacher judges that a child has practiced one piece enough, he gives the accompaniment tape for the piece and says to the child, "At the next lesson, please let me hear you play the piece with the accompaniment tape." The child can proceed to the next piece if he or she can play well enough with the accompaniment. This method has had a marvelous effect on the students' sensitivity for musical tempo and beat. It also enhances children's enthusiasm for music.

Practice With Me

Children's abilities are developed at home. So Suzuki teachers, in the classroom, teach children how to practice correctly at home. The teachers, therefore, have to study how to make the children's home practice joyful. For that purpose I made the tapes called "Practice With Me," and many students have used them effectively. I recorded my playing of each piece from the Suzuki School Books and my explanations on how to practice the piece at home joyously. At the top of the tape I talk to our young students, "Now let's practice together. I will repeat my performance as many times as you want to practice with me. When you become able to play this piece very well, please play again with the piano accompaniment." Each tape has the piano accompaniment part after my instruction. This series of the tapes for home practice is not only very helpful to parents who are at a loss as to how they should help their children practice at home, but also it brings effective results to children's development. This is one of the important features of the Suzuki Method.

Lessons In The Classroom

The most important thing in infant education is to make children motivated to learn. A teacher should try to do his best to make his class joyous and pleasant. We never scold children nor find faults with them. Who scolds his baby when it makes a mistake in speaking its mother tongue because of poor ability in speaking? It is natural that a baby cannot speak very well. In learning music, the same principle applies. Young children who are still poor in their ability of speaking, of course, cannot play musical instruments very well. So the teacher should have the children practice a familiar piece with him over and over again, sometimes saying jokingly, "You are doing very well, except for some bad points."

Needless to say, the responsibility to correct these faults is on the side of parents at home, and teachers in the classroom. In our institute three or four students are scheduled for the same time in each lesson. The teacher instructs one student at a time directly, while the other students observe. They can learn from observing others' lessons. Sometimes they can have a chance to study with more advanced students. They are probably affected and encouraged by the advanced students' performances.

This method develops children's abilities and helps children enjoy their lessons. Each lesson is not long. We teach just one vital point at a time to the student, so that he can practice it over and over again at home. We teach one point at one lesson thoroughly. If we do this, his abilities can be developed very highly. On the other hand, if we give two or three learning points at a time, children will surely fail to grasp the points. I have learned this through my experiences. Children can be greatly influenced by each other, so they have a tendency to lose their eagerness for learning when they are kept in a one-to-one-style lesson *between one teacher and one student.*

Solo Concert Day

The last week of every other month is the week for solo concert. There is no ordinary class this week. On Monday all the students of the Monday classes and their parents get together in a classroom for the concert. On Tuesday all the students of Tuesday classes and their parents get together, and so on.

On that day each student demonstrates the results of his two-month-long home practice with the accompaniment tapes. This concert is a very good chance for the students to show their improvement in front of their classmates and to learn from their frinds' performances. They enjoy these periodic concerts very much. Applause and praise given by their friends motivate them to practice more at home. I noticed, through my experiences, that this sort of activity is very helpful in developing enthusiasm for steady practice among young learners.

I recommend that you occasionally hold this sort of concert. A teacher might well choose some pieces for the concert a month or so ahead and make his students practice them. Then children can master two or three pieces thoroughly for a month, if the pieces are not long.

Group Lessons

Once a month at least, all the children in the class are called together, and they joyfully play together the pieces they have learned up to now. Through the group lessons they can effectively study musical beat, correct posture, beautiful tone, poise, etc.

These occasions are extremely effective, especially for small children, because they can play and learn with advanced students. Anyway, children like to play in a group and they learn, unconsciously, poise, musical beat, and how to make beautiful tone from the more advanced and excellently developed children.

Every year in March we hold a grand concert at the annual convention of the Japanese Talent Education Movement. Three thousand children from all over Japan perform together with perfect harmony without rehearsing beforehand. It is possible because the children have been trained through their usual lessons under the instruction of their regular teachers in their home towns all over Japan.

Presenting Graduation Tapes

Students of our system in Japan go through five graduation steps, from elementary to advanced. Each student submits his recorded tapes to me when applying for graduation from whatever level he is in. This system of assigning the graduation pieces has proved to be very effective in motivating students' learning, because children practice enthusiastically aiming at the next graduation level, and they do their best for it.

This year we numbered seven thousand nine hundred graduates in violin, piano, 'cello and flute. I listened to all these graduation tapes sent from the graduates all over Japan and carefully checked them all. Of course, it is the teacher in charge of the student who judges whether or not the student deserves to graduate from his level. I, as president of the Talent Education Institute, just authorize his graduation according to his teacher's recommendation. No student who submits the tape can fail to graduate. We make it a rule that graduation certificates are granted to all the students who submitted the tapes. Then the graduation concerts are held in many districts in Japan.

The purpose of this system is to stimulate students' learning motivation. I firmly believe this system is very effective for the purpose of motivation, so I hope eagerly that teachers instructing children through the Suzuki Method will use this system positively in many parts of the world.

Tonalization

The research and teaching of vocalization is the most important aspect of vocal music. It is said that the quality of teaching of vocalization shows the quality, whether superior or inferior, of the teacher.

Since I noticed this some time ago, I have been applying the idea to my violin teaching. Now I usually spend the first half of my individual lesson period each time on teaching the very basic techniques on how to produce beautiful and noble tone on the instrument, just as vocal music teachers do on vocalization. After that I give my student his lesson on the piece of music he is studying.

In vocal music teaching Vocalization is a technical term producing a beautiful voice, and the teaching method for it is established. We had no equivalent term, nor method for beautiful sound production from an instrument. However, I proposed to teachers of the Suzuki Method in the States that we should establish such a teaching method to produce beautiful tone and we should give it an appropriate name. Then they molded the new term, Tonalization. Since then I have been fond of using "tonalization", and I am emphasizing how to practice and teach beautiful tone production.

I have offered to the teachers in Japan what I have researched and developed on this subject. Now they also are teaching tonalization to their students, using the Research tapes on which I recorded the new procedures for it. I believe that these tapes are quite useful for the teachers to use in their further study on this subject. I hope from the bottom of my heart that a finer method of teaching tonalization—— one that will be the finest—— will be established as soon as possible through exchanging better ideas about it between teachers in the world and through cooperative studies on this subject. As a matter of fact, I can tell you that the students learning from teachers who have pro-

foundly reserched tonalization are all gaining excellent performance ability. It is very important for teachers to develop their students' abilities by teaching them how to produce correct and beautiful tone on the strings from the beginning of their learning.

The Research Tapes For Teachers

For some time, we Suzuki teachers in Japan have had research tapes which involve newly devised teaching procedures, techniques, instructions of tonalization and studies made by myself and other teachers. Using these tapes, we are endeavoring to research better ways for teaching children more effectively. They are really helpful for that purpose. In this way teachers all over Japan can gain the latest information and teaching methods. They also can learn greatly from the results of research made one after another by other teachers.

I believe that this "research–tape–system" is functioning as one of the most productive tactics for promoting our movement. I have a sincere desire for teachers all over the world, using the Suzuki Method, to establish an organization for offering successful education to every child in many parts of the world. We should be able to expect great progress for our movement if we have such a powerful organization and can offer the research tapes to all members as well as to those in Japan.

The Suzuki Method is not a fixed method, but is continuously progressing day by day. It is seeking better and newer ways to develop children's abilities to a much higher level in a joyous natural atmosphere in the easiest way possible. Every child can be well educated. Every child has such wonderful potential and powerful "life force" in him. Now, teachers from all over the world, let us study together how to nurture our children correctly and how to develop their abilities to the most splendid level.

From 196 children in 1952 to over 9000 in 1980, the candidates for "Graduation" exemplify the growth and quality of the Talent Education movement in Japan. Not shown on the graph are graduates in cello, 158; flute, 49, and viola, 2.

Lists of graduating students on violin and piano in each age group in 1980

Violin

Grade		Age 3	4	5	6	7	8	9	10	11	12	over 13	Total
1	Gossec···Gavotte	6	87	313	505	328	208	111	44	23	13	16	1,654
2	Bach···Bourrée		14	65	182	265	281	190	114	54	26	25	1,216
3	Vivaldi···Concerto g minor		1	16	45	84	169	168	151	85	39	50	808
4	Corelli···La Folia			4	19	35	80	133	138	120	84	122	735
5	Bach···Concerto a minor			2	2	14	31	61	82	54	38	77	361
6	Mozart···Concerto No. 4				1	0	1	10	11	16	20	98	157
7	Mozart···Rondo						1	1	3	18	20	82	125
													5,056

Piano

Grade		Age 3	4	5	6	7	8	9	10	11	12	over 13	Total
1	Bach···Minuet No.2	1	39	164	357	410	375	281	218	138	74	56	2,113
2	Bach···2 Minuets and Gique			7	23	71	124	172	146	139	115	148	945
3	Mozart···Sonata K. 331				0	5	11	35	76	77	67	115	386
4	Bach···Italian Concerto				1	0	4	7	18	22	31	116	199
5	Mozart···Coronation Concerto								6	4	13	55	78
6	Bach···Partita No.1							1	1	9	10	45	66
7	Beethoven···Sonata Appassionata							1	0	0	1	11	13
													3,800

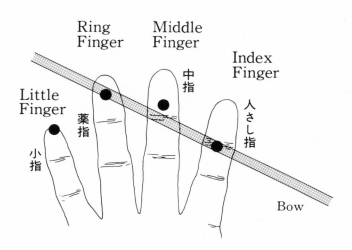

- The points for holding the bow.

●弓を持つ指の場所

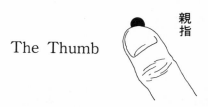

The Thumb

Suzuki indicates points on the fingers and thumb where contact with the bow is to be felt. To experience and experiment with the feel of the stick and the hand as Suzuki suggests can produce insights into how he views tone production.

Holding the Bow

by Evelyn Hermann

Of the technics which Dr. Suzuki espouses regarding the art of violin playing, the least understood seems to be the bow hold. In the Western world, many violin teachers have adopted nearly every part of Suzuki's approach except the right hand configuration. Suzuki feels that the bow grip which he advocates is essential to the production of the tonal quality which has become identified as the "Talent Education" sound.

One of the most important parts of the bow hold is the placement of the thumb. This produces "thumb power." Recently the author was working with some young students at a Suzuki Institute. After showing the children the bow hold, a very young Japanese boy, whose first name just happened to be Shinichi, stated succinctly, "If your thumb is wrong, you can't get your elbow down. If your thumb is right, you can't get your elbow too high."

I replied, "Thank you for the lesson."

Observe the pictures of Dr. Suzuki's hand. First the student makes a fox head with his right hand. Form this by extending your fingers and thumb straight out. Slowly bring the middle fingers and the thumb together, touching the inside corner of the thumb between the middle fingers at the joint of the end phalanx. The thumb points to the ring finger. The touch is very light. Keep the "ears" up

(the index and little fingers). Keep the hand relaxed. Does this not look like a fox? (Photo 1)

Using the same hand position, insert a pencil between the thumb and middle fingers. (Photo 2) Drop the "ears" lightly onto the pencil. When this looks like photos 3, 4, and 5, try it on the bow.

The thumb placement on the bow is as follows: Place the inside corner of the thumb halfway on the frog and halfway on the stick. (Photo 6) The two middle fingers are almost perpendicular to the stick rather than at an angle. (Photo 7) Beginners will be playing in the upper part of the bow. Therefore, their thumb will be almost straight. The thumb bends only when the elbow takes over in the lower part of the bow.

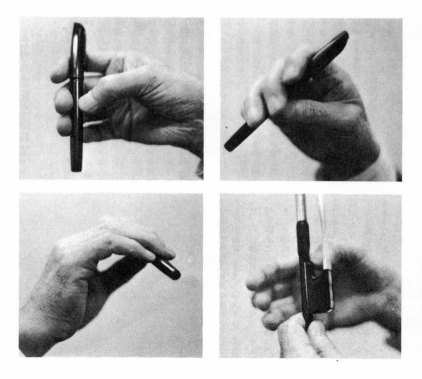

The initial hold itself is only a part of the concept. The thumb and middle fingers carry the bow at all times. No weight is added with the index finger. Dr. Suzuki says, "Play with the hair, not the stick." Also be careful not to wrap the index finger around the stick to such an extent that it pulls the middle fingers from their correct position.

The final point is very important for tone control. The down-bow is carried by the thumb and the middle finger. The up-bow is carried by thumb and ring finger. There should be no excessive finger action. The only perceived hand movement takes place in the thumb. It will bend slightly when playing near the frog. If the thumb makes a slight turn from the up-bow to the down-bow, be certain that it turns toward the hand. When it turns out, the position is lost. The wrist is relaxed and bends as needed, but it has no power.

The entire hand must be strong, but relaxed; strong when needed, but without tension. Any tension is telescoped to the bow and affects the tone.

Many young beginning students are introduced to a bow hold in which the thumb is placed on the outside of the frog, directly opposite the location for the thumb in its regular position. The inside corner of the thumb tip is placed half on the silver ferrule and half on the hair of the bow. It remains there until the teacher ascertains that the hand is reliably rounded, stable and free of excessive tension. The change to the traditional grip could occur any time during the first year or as late as the third year of study.

Having the thumb on the outside of the frog in the early stages has several benefits. The primary reason is for the increased stability given to the hand which is unaccustomed to controling a pencil-thin stick. In addition, the visability of the thumb allows the teacher to check its position easily. The more open contour of the hand promotes curved fingers and less tension.

The Answers I Discovered During the Past Forty Years and My Future Hope and Dream

by Shinichi Suzuki

1. The discovery of the "Law of Ability." One must understand the principle of this law in education.
2. The work of the living soul. The preservation of Health and Youth.
3. Abilities are developed physiologically due to the work of the living soul.

We must study the educational system of the mother's tongue method. We must study together to find the condition in which all children can be developed and educated. We must cooperate to promote this movement with respect, friendship, and understanding in order to find the result, not only in music but in all other fields of education. Let us cooperate to fulfill the dream of making a new era in which all children on earth can receive the right education.

"Probably music will save the world."

This statement of Mr. Pablo Casals is our mutual mission.

Bibliography

Cook, Clifford. *Suzuki Education in Action.* Smithtown, New York: Exposition Press. 1970.

Honda, Masaaki. *A Program for Early Development.* Tokyo: Early Development Association. n.d., circa 1970.

Smith, Bradley. *Japan: A History in Art.* New York: Doubleday and Co. 1964.

Suzuki, Shinichi. *Nurtured By Love.* Smithtown, New York: Exposition Press. 1969.

DATE DUE

NOV 1 1 1983			
NOV 2 6 1983			
OCT 1 1 1984			
10/8/86			
OCT 0 2 1988			
FEB 1 4 1995			
FEB 2 1 1995			
MAY 1 6 2000			
FEB 1 7 2010			
GAYLORD			PRINTED IN U.S.A